SEIZING CONTROL:

THE INTERNATIONAL MARKET POWER OF COOPERATIVES
BY LEE EGERSTROM, DR. GERT VAN DIJK & IR. PIETER BOS

FEATURING
DOUGLASS C. NORTH, WERNER GROSSKOPF,
JERKER NILSSON, JESPER STRANDSKOV,
LEE EGERSTROM, MICHAEL L. COOK,
ROEL IN 'T VELD, VERNON W. RUTTAN,
DAVID HUGHES, ARIE VAN DER ZWAN, GERT VAN DIJK

LONE OAK PRESS, LTD.

SEIZING CONTROL:
THE INTERNATIONAL MARKET POWER OF COOPERATIVES
BY LEE EGERSTROM, DR. GERT VAN DIJK & IR. PIETER BOS

FEATURING
DOUGLASS C. NORTH, WERNER GROSSKOPF, JERKER NILSSON,
JESPER STRANDSKOV, LEE EGERSTROM, MICHAEL L. COOK,
ROEL IN 'T VELD, VERNON W. RUTTAN,
DAVID HUGHES, ARIE VAN DER ZWAN, GERT VAN DIJK

ENGLISH EDITION PUBLISHED BY
LONE OAK PRESS, LTD.
304 11TH AVENUE SE, ROCHESTER, MINNESOTA 55904 507-280-6557

First English Edition
ISBN NUMBER 1-883477-14-X
LIBRARY OF CONGRESS CARD CATALOG NUMBER 96-78130

First Dutch Edition ISBN 90-9009020-7
Published in Dutch, December 1995 by
Campina Milkunie, Postbus 2100, 5300 CC Zaltbommel, Nederlands
Telephone 0418-571300 Fax 0418-540116

Seizing Control

TABLE OF CONTENTS

PREFACE

The circumstances, or environment, in which agriculture and the food sectors operate have changed dramatically in recent years, and these changes continue to unfold. Many businesses are being reorganized, restructured and renewed. The business literature indicates that considerable attention is being given to the causes, methods and results of reorganization efforts. But the cooperative form of business is receiving far less attention in financial, economic and academic circles.

During periods of change, broad discussions, analysis and synthesis are necessary for successful renewal of different types of enterprise. It is therefore useful to know how matters are discussed in other countries; what problems are being observed elsewhere, and what solutions are being discovered and put to work. In part, observation of problems and the study of possible methods of renewal demand an international scientific approach. Beyond finding common ground in these observations, however, there are aspects of business environments specific to cultures that are not widely transferable. Both areas of general and specific studies are yielding important information for organizations contemplating change.

The timing for such studies is important as cooperatives are now crossing national frontiers and encountering cultures and business law in other countries that need to be properly understood.

Thus, a warning is in order: This book does not provide ready answers to any cooperative organization's problems; it wasn't the editors' intention. The book is intended to broaden and deepen discussions on what the future holds for cooperatives. In doing so, there are different socio-economic sciences concerned with the organization and behavior of different types of business. These socio-economic disciplines can contribute to the discussion of cooperatives while throwing light on marketing and commercial issues. The willingness of outside business and economics authorities to discuss cooperatives within an international framework may stimulate broader interest in cooperatives' significance, and is much appreciated by the editors.

Care was taken in selecting various experts to interview for this project. Through the efforts of Dr. Gert van Dijk, director of the National Cooperative Council for Agriculture & Horticulture (NCR) in the Netherlands and a professor at Wageningen Agricultural University; and Lee Egerstrom, an American journalist and author on topics of agriculture and trade, we have succeeded in drawing together a team of internationally recognized academics to share their thoughts and observations for this book.

Van Dijk, Egerstrom and I have edited the texts. Some interviews were conducted by Dr. Jan Werts, the former editor-in-chief of the Dutch journal *Oogst* (Harvest) and its current correspondent at the European Union in Brussels. Leo Klep has provided professional translation services for texts. Mrs. Nicole van der Zijden of the National Cooperative Council arranged interviews and administered the flow of copy.

Ir. Pieter Bos

Pieter Bos, 53, is president of two Waterboards in the Netherlands and is former editor-in-chief of the farming journals **Boerderij** (Farm), the largest agricultural weekly in the Netherlands and **Oogst** (Harvest), the farmers weekly of the National Farmeres Organization in the Netherlands. In addition to running a consultancy, he is a free lance agricultural journalist.

INTRODUCTION TO THE ENGLISH LANGUAGE EDITION

The reasons for the book, and the foundation support for its publishing, are explained in the preceding Preface and in the following Foreword and Dedication. But as Pieter Bos has already explained, changes are occurring to rural economies and cooperative business structures worldwide; it is therefore our hope that this book, in English, will be of benefit to farmers, cooperative business people, rural development planners and educators in several countries.

Some minor changes have been made from the original Dutch text. More footnotes have been added to explain concepts or national phenomena for international readers. And the sequence of chapters has been shuffled in an attempt to package the different essays in categories for the convenience of readers and researchers. Having done this, it should be noted that chapters profiling Professors Ruttan and In 't Veld could easily have been placed in other categories.

We, the writers and editors of this book, salute the Dutch cooperative Campina Melkunie and the Nationale Cooperatieve Raad (NCR) for their foresight in launching this project. We also salute Harvest States Cooperatives, Farmland Industries, the St. Paul Bank for Cooperatives, Cenex and the Saskatchewan Wheat Pool in North America for their recognition of the project's importance. They supported the Minnesota Association of Cooperatives and Lone Oak Press in bringing this language edition to a wider world audience. We owe special thanks to Jim Erickson, a gifted editor with an eye for syntax and pronouns, for reading the translated manuscript; to Inkie Rutgers, whose linguistic skills helped paraphrase some unique Dutch terms in English; to Ray Howe, publisher of Lone Oak Press; and especially to Allen Gerber, president of the Minnesota Association of Cooperatives, for their support and encouragement. Finally, we must express our gratitude to the profound American, Dutch, British-Canadian, Swedish, Danish and

German economists and business professors profiled herein for their patience and cooperation in this project.

We are pleased to report the Dutch edition has been well received in the Netherlands and in neighboring countries of Northern Europe. Perhaps the most dramatic response has been at Nijenrode University, the Netherlands School of Business. Nijenrode has since appointed Professor Arie Van der Zwan, whose prophetic vision is profiled in Chapter 10, as dean of the business school. Now, under Dean Van der Zwan's leadership, Nijenrode is establishing a Center for Entrepreneurship and an Institute for Cooperative Entrepreneurship that begin operations with the 1967-68 academic year. This innovative effort will link faculties from the graduate school of business with agricultural economists, cooperative business experts and various social scientists to develop curricula to educate tomorrow's rural development and cooperative business leaders.

Lee Egerstrom
Gert van Dijk
Pieter Bos

FOREWORD AND DEDICATION

The net turnover of Dutch agricultural cooperatives, excluding Rabobank, is NLG 40 billion, or approximately U.S. $25 billion, which is no mean sum in a nation of about 15 million people. About 6,500 cooperative businesses are registered with Dutch chambers of commerce. At the same time, education, scientific research, financial institutions and politics pay hardly any attention to the cooperative as a form of business.

This lack of attention, and the unclear image of cooperatives, hinder their renewal. Despite this lack of scientific and political action, cooperatives in the Netherlands are changing dramatically to prepare themselves for tomorrow's markets. Like other types of enterprise, cooperatives are confronted with change: market concentration, internationalization, new modes of finance and the limiting of membership.

Against this background, the dairy cooperative Campina Melkunie launched a survey of thinking about cooperatives among an international team of academics. Some top economists and business professors were approached and their thoughts have been recorded in this book. We hope it will stimulate closer consideration of the phenomenon of cooperation among academics.

In Dedication

Willem Overmars: 11 years of dairy cooperative leadership

The first copy of the Dutch version of this book was presented to Mr. Willem Overmars, the retiring chairman of our Central Directorate, on 29 November 1995. During the 11 years of his chairmanship, Campina Melkunie's turnover and profitability grew, and there was healthy development in internationalization, internal organization and strategic thinking.

This book is dedicated to Willem Overmars for his impressive contribution to the development of Campina Melkunie. We of the Dutch dairy cooperative sector owe him a great debt of gratitude.

P.J. Loonen
Chairman, board of Directors and the Supervisory Board
Campina Melkunie

DIRECTORY

PART ONE: ASSESSING CHANGE IN THE GLOBAL FOOD SYSTEM AND ITS IMPACT ON FARMERS

1. PROFESSOR DOUGLASS NORTH

Adjusting to a changing world: A process of elimination for evaluating institutions, cooperative organizations; a strategy for reducing transaction costs.

The agriculture sector's political power has grown in recent history while the number of farmers and agribusinesses has declined. This position of power could change, says the Nobel laureate economic historian. And it most likely is changing. As a consequence, Dr. North suggests a method of exclusion, or elimination, for cooperatives and agricultural organizations to evaluate whether they can still change their business environment within the political economy. If they cannot, farmers and their firms will have to draw their own conclusions from changes occurring in world markets to decide the future form of their organizations. Whatever the outcome of that exercise, North says cooperatives can generally reduce transaction costs for their members.

2. PROFESSOR DAVID HUGHES

A new look at countervailing power: Consumers offer new opportunities for farmers and their cooperatives.

Power lies with the consumer, not with the large retail chains, insists the food industry expert from Wye College, the University of London. Despite the enormous concentration of power in a few retail chains operating in most developed countries, Professor Hughes has a strong conviction that consumer power offers cooperatives new opportunities. The large chains must differentiate their product offerings by introducing new products under their own brand names. To profit from this opportunity, cooperatives need to be large enough to supply the chains directly. That shouldn't be a problem, Hughes adds, if farmers combine forces.

3. JOURNALIST LEE EGERSTROM

The need for a course correction in world agriculture: Horizontal expansion is disastrous for rural life.

Cooperatives in Northern Europe, in general, have gained a stronger role in handling members' raw produce and in initial stages of processing than have their North American counterparts. In contrast, American and Canadian farmers are far more dependent on world commodity prices. The farm income difference between good and bad years is therefore much greater, observes the American journalist, and this instability leads to enormous increases in the scale of farm operations. Horizontal expansion of farms has been disastrous for the American rural economy and rural society, he says, and is causing renewed interest in aggressive, vertically-structured cooperatives. Egerstrom sees horizontal expansion as an emerging threat to Europe and a force holding back rural economic development in South America, Africa and in the former centrally-planned economies.

PART TWO: ASSESSING COOPERATIVE STRENGTHS WHEN APPROACHING CHANGE

4. PROFESSOR ROEL IN 'T VELD

A closer look at society: Cooperatives as an organizational form for the future.

Collective values are the basis for interaction among members in a cooperative. But these values are being influenced by changes in the "value-set" of society and by changes in the cooperative enterprise, observes the Dutch business professor. Professor in 't Veld raises several questions on how cooperatives are adjusting to these changing values. For instance, how critical is the relationship between values and increases in the scale of operations? Is there a certain limit of scale from which the basis for the values crumbles away? How can you determine the value-set of a cooperative? What conclusions can you draw from that, and what can you do about it? The cooperative is an organizational form with a future, insists Dr. in 't Veld, who sees the value-set of society again moving in the direction of cooperatives.

5. PROFESSOR VERNON RUTTAN

A look at induced innovation: The role of resources, culture, technology and institutions in changing markets and changing cooperatives.

Professor Ruttan and his Japanese colleague, Professor Hayami, pioneered the induced innovation theory that explains the origin of technical and institutional renewal. The Ruttan-Hayami model demonstrates the theory by representing the relations between factors that induce change. Ruttan, the Von Humboldt Prize laureate and advisor to governments and international institutions on economic development, explains why agriculture and cooperatives in developed countries are exploring prospects for change. The model also helps frame the discussion of cooperatives that follows this chapter.

PART THREE: PERSPECTIVES ON CHANGE AND GLOBAL MARKET POWER

6. PROFESSOR JESPER STRANDSKOV

A view from Denmark: First merge nationally, then penetrate the entire production-marketing chain.

Cooperatives face competition from two sides: first, by the cheaper retail chain brands available from supermarkets; second, by the aggressive brand marketing of large multinational companies. Cooperatives must therefore gain control of the entire production and marketing chain for their produce, says Dr. Strandskov, the noted Danish business professor and advisor to Danish cooperatives. To do so, the cooperatives must combine forces through mergers. Dr. Strandskov sketches four models with which Danish cooperatives can expand internationally and develop new products.

7. PROFESSOR JERKER NILSSON

A view from Sweden: Involvement of members is the most precious asset of the cooperative.

The so-called "agency theory" is too readily applied to cooperatives, warns Dr. Nilsson, the Swedish economist and international cooperative business expert. He notes there is confusion between cooperatives and the Swedish government regarding the role of cooperatives as Sweden readies itself to be more competitive in the European Union. But Nilsson stresses that transaction costs show there is more involved in cooperatives than simply making profits. The cooperatives must be seen as working for members, and must be financed and controlled by members. And on the other hand, cooperatives should pay members interest on their individual capital invested or retained in the cooperative, he says. Finally, this academic champion of cooperatives says the firms that no longer offer benefits to members should be closed down.

8. PROFESSOR WERNER GROSSKOPF

A view from Germany: How farmer-directors can influence strategic decision-making.

Internationalization of the cooperative is necessary and unavoidable, but it creates problems for the governance of the organization. Besides financial aspects, control over strategic decisions also becomes a problem. Dr. Grosskopf offers some suggestions to help farmers keep control at an acceptable level while gaining the sophisticated information they need for governance. The greatest danger in internationalization is a gap developing between management and members, he says. Therefore, Grosskopf suggests that cooperatives devoted to primary production in the European Union can best be internationalized by uniting under a joint holding company. This model has application for U.S.-Canadian cooperatives as well.

9. PROFESSOR MICHAEL L. COOK

A view from North America: New Generation Cooperatives as an alternative approach.

Farmers wanting to move farther up the food chain now have convenient and successful models to follow, but it requires a change in "mind-set," or thinking, about the farmers' role and obligations in a cooperative organization. Professor Michael Cook, the American expert on cooperatives who helped originate the concept of New Generation Cooperatives, says new, value-added firms represent this change in mind-set. The value-added cooperatives do not want to operate as trading cooperatives for primary produce. Rather, they operate as investor-driven enterprises that only take produce from their members that they can ultimately sell. Most years, these New Generation Cooperatives can provide members a better return on investment and labor than the commodity markets. And, Cook says, these investor-driven organizations work as a model for cooperatives that wish to play a role internationally.

PART FOUR: DEFINING LOCAL FARM AND COMMUNITY INTERESTS IN NEW, GLOBAL MARKETS

10. PROFESSOR ARIE VAN DER ZWAN

A look at global change and local society: New cooperative vigor and cottage industry as weapons of opportunity for producers, workers, communities.

"Unbridled" expansion and internationalization dislocate the local labor market, says Professor van der Zwan, a leading Dutch observer of business and public administration. He expects the pendulum will swing again, to reverse current trends, through government policy. But another response can be the formation of new cooperatives that combine new forms of cottage industry and trade. Upgrade your own raw produce: that is the trend, according to Van der Zwan, and the time is ripe to do so. The market is asking for more exclusive products. With modern technology, return to a highly developed level of cottage industry is possible.

11. PROFESSOR GERT VAN DIJK

Epilogue:

The changing theoretical perspective of cooperatives and markets.

Cooperatives throughout the developed, or industrialized world, are exploring change and evaluating the need for change. This is especially so in the Netherlands. The theoretical perspective of cooperatives has changed, observes Dr. van Dijk. Cooperative management needs to consider the influence of members, issues of accountability, and thorny questions about investment and risk. In short, cooperatives must explore what institutional and organizational changes are needed from a broader framework than in the past. The director of the Dutch National Cooperative Council and professor of Cooperative Theory, Van Dijk reflects on matters raised by contributors in the preceding chapters. And he distinguishes four generations of cooperatives in order to discuss current trends.

PART ONE: ASSESSING CHANGE IN THE GLOBAL FOOD SYSTEM AND ITS IMPACT ON FARMERS

DOUGLASS C. NORTH

Professor Douglass C. North, 74, the recipient of the Nobel Prize for Economics in 1993, currently holds the Henry R. Luce chair for Law and Liberty and is professor of Economics and History at Washington University, St. Louis, Missouri, in the United States.

His diverse work in economic history focuses on the role of institutions in economic development, the definition and measuring of transaction costs, and their relationship to economic growth. In addition, his published works have explored the causes of institutional change.

The Nobel laureate has previously taught at the University of California at Berkeley, the University of Washington at Seattle, Rice University in Texas, Stanford University in California, and at the University of Cambridge in the United Kingdom. He has also lectured at prominent universities in Europe, North America, South America, China, Hong Kong and Japan.

Professor North is currently engaged in research regarding property law, culture and public policy, free-rider problems, growth of government, economic and social change, and the theory of institutional change.

ADJUSTING TO A CHANGING WORLD:

A process of elimination for evaluating institutions, cooperative organizations; a strategy for reducing transaction costs.

By Lee Egerstrom

Professor Douglass North leaned back in his chair, rubbed his chin, and let out a gentle laugh. "Frankly," he said, "I'm more familiar with

Dutch developments between the 15th and 17th Centuries. But I think I know a process of elimination the Dutch might use to evaluate where they are today."

It is a process that complements the work of other economists and business experts cited in this book. And while he cites Dutch historical experiences, cognizant that the first edition of this book was to be published in the Netherlands, the professor's approach to evaluation is equally germane to other highly developed agricultural and industrial countries.

A Nobel laureate (1993), Professor North is best known for historical economics in which he studies the role of institutions and their influence on economic performance over periods of time.(1) An historical perspective undoubtedly helps explain why world agriculture may now be at a turning point in history that will shape future institutions and farmers' organizations. And, he says, today's alert agricultural organizations may be evaluating options for the 21st Century just as Dutch farmers, traders, shippers and government officials undoubtedly did in the earlier centuries when they rose to economic prominence in Europe.

The historical background starts from the fact agriculture has emerged as one of the most regulated and subsidized industries in the political economy of nations, he says as he begins explaining his process. "Everywhere in the world, where agriculture becomes a minority, its political power grows. U.S. farm policies, the European Union farm policies, reveal that power. Japan is another good example," he says.

Over time, he adds, the institutions created by this political power begins to warp, or bend, as other interest groups "tie" in with the government programs. "It's happening to agriculture in Europe and it's happening in America, although it appears it is only beginning to in Japan," he says.

These "tie-ins," as he calls them, may be shown by the American sugar price support program. "I just love using the sugar program in lectures for my classes because it makes such a good example," he says. "Professor Anne Krueger wrote a great paper on the political economy of sugar some years ago that shows it started in the 1930s as a way to help Cuba.(2) That purpose disappeared (with President Fidel Castro's revolution), but the program stays. It effectively sets the world price for sugar and it gives corn processors a target to shoot at with sweetener substitutes," he says.

"One of the points Anne Krueger cites is that the sugar program now gives an average of $136,000 a year in benefits to a small group of producers. If the consumers knew this they would revolt!" (3)

On a parallel course, American farmers were mostly "free traders" in the 19th Century when a majority of Americans lived on farms, says Professor North. Modern programs for agricultural production and trade started in the 1930s, when the farm population was declining, and continue on to today. Farm numbers have continued to decline and the U.S. farm population is now down to about 2 percent of the American population. These programs were under attack in the U.S. Congress in the fall of 1995 for ideological as well as budgetary reasons. North did not know at the time of this interview that Congress would begin scaling back and eliminating federal support to farm production. Regardless, he says, "Farmers have acquired enormous power for their numbers!" And, he adds, benefits of the U.S. farm program have rarely helped the small farmers who were experiencing the most financial stress. They are the farmers the general public – taxpayers – would be most willing to support.

Modern European farm policies are of post-World War II origin. They started out serving broader public interests, he says. They, too, evolved into more narrowly focused support for farmers. And if anyone doubts the power of European farmers, he adds, "Just watch French politics."

Now, however, other voices from other interest groups are being heard. Certainly, the voices of consumers wanting access to the global marketplace are being heard. And expansion of the European Union brings new voices to policy debates in Brussels. Balancing the interests of diverse groups is causing the general decline in income support for farmers at the same time production of major commodities, such as milk, remains under production controls that limit farmers' income potential. Most likely, he says, these changes in policies are not driven by economic considerations.

Process of Elimination

Given the current environment for agriculture, he says, farmers should begin the process by evaluating what their cooperatives and organizations can accomplish in the political economy. "Institutions are the rules of the game. I wouldn't assume that one needs to change the organizations to adjust to changing institutions until I explored what can be done with the institutions," he says.

Thus starts the process of elimination, the economic historian says. Dutch farmers, for instance, should consider if going to The Hague can bring relief in the political economy, as it did in earlier times. If power in agriculture's political economy has shifted to Brussels, then what can be accomplished within the European Union? The first question is whether the farmers, through their cooperatives, are still capable of changing their business environment. "It's not clear the organization must change but the institutions are changing."

As a result, he says, the cooperative may not need to change "internally" even though it changes "externally" to participate in the global market. Such changes don't simply apply to agriculture, he notes. All producers or manufacturers who want to be players in international markets are facing the same questions. So, through a process of elimination, organizations – such as cooperatives or other firms – should be able to define what is required for restructuring or changing their organizations.

"Research is part of the process. Not just new products but new ways of marketing. Not just in technology but in finding new or niche markets," he says.

Shifts in Policies

Changes in agriculture policy cannot be divorced from the rest of the political economy that has evolved after World War II, says the expert on institutional change. What occurred to agriculture policies – or institutions – has also occurred to other segments of living and industry in most industrialized nations, he notes. Commerce and industry have been wrapped up in the general growth of government. In Europe, this growth has come in both national governments and in multinational governments such as the European Union.

Therefore, he doubts consumers are directly the driving force behind changes occurring to world markets. Competition from other players, including many new ones from fast-growing economies in Asia and parts of South America, is causing change. "Competition is really the driving force. Consumers are the happy recipients of changes in policies." (4)

What governments and their taxpayers are looking at are costs associated with policies that evolved in recent decades, he says. What started out as a "safety net" under agriculture and other segments of national societies grew to being broader programs for welfare concerns and redistributing incomes. These programs didn't fail; they succeeded in meeting their original objectives, he says. It is the growth and evolution of these programs into broader institutions that are causing nations to question future public spending.

Evolution of government programs to serve broader purposes is "a little like killing the goose that laid the golden egg," Professor North says. The Dutch have experience with such actions.

The European Union's Common Agriculture Policy isn't designed to encourage efficiency, for instance. "Efficiency may happen. But it's an accident if it does!" Instead, it seeks political objectives for Europe that may actually be holding back the Dutch and others in Northern Europe, he says.

"The Netherlands was the first modern country for economic growth, producing for the world market. The English learned everything from the Netherlands. They even imported a king," he recalls jokingly. And, in another time, when Phillip II of Spain tried to tax the Dutch trading success, "they (the Dutch) threw him off."

Professor North, who was a visiting scholar at the Hoover Institution at Stanford University in California at the time of this interview, laughs as he gives this playful account of Dutch history. But it is relevant to his current work: he is involved in research on the growth of government and economic organization in history, and he is attempting to find ways that economists can penetrate cultures to measure economic performance of institutions.

Transaction Costs

The costs of operating and maintaining institutions are growing, Professor North notes, and bureaucracies have grown especially large. But the economic historian isn't against all rules and regulations.

Governments are the primary enforcer of rules of trade, or "rules of the game," as he calls them. The cost of these enforcement services, both official and informal, are called "transaction costs" by economists. Between 1870 and the 1970s, he says, transaction costs rose from about 25 percent of Gross National Product in advanced countries to 45 percent.(5) Caught up in these costs are lawyers fees, litigation in courts to enforce contracts, insurance premium payments to reduce risks, trade brokerage services and a wide range of business services that either help trade or reduce risks of trade. Institutional support of trade, such as regulations that assure quality of products and thus increase buyers' confidence, is also part of transaction costs.

Transaction costs are still rising, Professor North says. Modern technology, such as computers and fax machines, is adding to these costs even as it is expanding trade and thus contributing to greater economic growth. He now estimates that transaction costs have or will soon surpass 50 percent of Gross National Product in industrialized countries.

"The rise in transaction costs I've cited made possible the use of modern technology.

"If I were in a Dutch cooperative, I'd be explaining this to the members," he says. Providing transaction cost services for food company customers and consumers offers growth potential for farmer-owned businesses, he adds. An enormous part of government costs is now related to services for enforcing rules and regulations. By removing risks and assuring quality, organizations such as cooperatives can take over some of the functions of existing institutions.

"The computer is the biggest thing to reduce transaction costs I've ever seen," he says. It is a tool that can be used by anyone; not just government or the service industries.

Norms of Behavior

Closely tied to transaction costs are norms of behavior, he says. An academic colleague at the University of Arizona (USA) and he have worked with college students on an experimental game trying to determine when the student-player may be tempted to cheat a business partner and when that same student is inclined to make certain all aspects of the hypothetical contract are fulfilled, or completed.

The exercise has been fun, he says, but it hasn't produced definitive results for academic study to this point. One signal has come from the students, however; the game's players are far more likely to adhere to all aspects of the "contract" if there is an intention to keep a trading relationship in the future. Corners may be cut if the game's players believe they are negotiating a one-time deal.

This is part of an effort by Professor North and other researchers to probe into culture for measuring economic performance. Economists don't normally do this, he admits. Anthropologists, sociologists and other researchers from the social sciences usually study culture and its impact on behavior. "But they don't usually look at economic performance the way we economists want to," he says.

How soon a method for doing so may be found isn't known and is beyond speculation. Professor North says he's got a lot of research to "keep me busy so I won't have to retire." But whatever he and his academic colleagues do discover will also shed light on future opportunities for cooperatives and farmers.

This research may reveal, in part, why cooperative businesses function with success in Northern Europe when they aren't a widely used form of business ownership in Southern Europe. The same is true in different states of the United States, where immigrants have duplicated cooperative structures in some areas and not in others. The result in both Europe and North America is uneven and led to different achievements in economic development.

The same research may help explain why economic development is currently rapid in parts of East Asia when it's practically non-existent in parts of sub-Sahara Africa, he says. Equally important, he adds, it may reveal why an entrepreneurial spirit is evident in China when communism all but destroyed it in the former Soviet Union.

"The questions become, why do some people cooperate – and I don't mean cooperative businesses now – and why is cooperation nearly impossible elsewhere? There are some good studies that have been done, such as comparing the Genoese traders with the Moorish kingdom. But there's a lot to be discovered," he says.

In some ways, cooperative businesses in Northern Europe are like kinship groups in olden times. Cooperating, people are part of "personal" business exchange. In less personal business arrangements, and where business is tightly controlled by authoritarian regimes, merchants were involved in "impersonal" exchange. Some scholars talk about Calvinist or religious influences on the norms of behavior, and that can't be dismissed, he says. But the Netherlands' experience with cooperative businesses shows there isn't a Catholic-Protestant split on economic cooperation.

What isn't easily explained is how market imperfections are built into the transaction costs of different cultures, he adds. In some nations, all economic growth gets deposited in Swiss bank accounts by corrupt rulers and no economic progress is observed by the population. In other countries, "even where there is local corruption, there are incentives built in to promote entrepreneurship.

"I think we economists have to look deeper into culture to understand economic performance," he says.

Regardless how soon such research bears fruit, the Dutch farmers' demonstrated abilities to cooperative should help reduce transaction costs between them and their worldwide customers, he says.(6) And this next achievement, too, can serve as a model for farmers in other nations who have learned to cooperate for common marketing aims.

Needs for Change

"If institutional change gives rise to new opportunities, or raises problems, an organization will either change or perish," Professor North says. "It's why the Dutch cooperatives have a bright future."

Like all organizations, cooperatives don't need to resemble a U-shape diagram that has marked many businesses. There will be rapid growth, then a leveling off and a sharp decline in performance if adjustments aren't made. Management and employees couldn't save a buggy manufacturing firm after the automobile age, he says, but the firm could grow and prosper if it started making automobiles.

Two industries in the United States provide examples of change that deserve attention by Northern European farmers, he says. One is the steel industry that was failing even with government assistance in the early 1980s, and the other was the declining American computer software industry that was being over taken by Japanese and Asian competition in the mid- and late-1980s.

"Today, we've got new technology, a string of steel mini-mills that make steel in a more efficient way, and our steel industry is strong and exporting throughout the world. And our software manufacturing is back on top," he says. Even the American auto industry has rebounded, he added. "All have evolved and are giving the Japanese a run for their money," he says.

As a result, he notes, the U-shape model of mature businesses isn't holding true for some of America's most "mature" industries.

In general, he said, organizations that are successful and don't fear a lot of competition are resistant to change and can be tripped up by changes in markets or institutions, he adds. "What's happening is global marketing that is really evolving, not just for agriculture but for all products.

"The Dutch are ahead of the world in asking what must they do. This changes how the players (Dutch farmers) perceive the game because they are looking at how to maintain the success of their industry, not only against new competition but different competitors."

Chapter Footnotes

1. North, Douglass C., with Davis, Lance E. Institutional Change and American Economic Growth. Cambridge University Press (1971); and North, Douglass C. Institutions, Institutional Change and Economic Performance. Cambridge University Press (1990).

2. Professor Anne O. Krueger has held economics posts at several American universities and is a former vice president for economics at The World Bank. The paper cited is out of print but was published as part of an occasional paper series by the National Bureau of Economic Research.

3. This point is debated, however, even among some economists. While most observers of trade policy agree with Dr. North's argument, exact costs to consumers are difficult to factor. The sugar policy does remove volatile run-ups in prices that mark the volatile coffee, cocoa and other specialty crops markets that prove, over time, to be extremely sensitive to world weather.

4. This observation contrasts slightly with the consumer-driven theory offered by Professor Hughes in another chapter. However, Hughes and North arrive at the same destination: competition is providing more products, and consumers want even more.

5. North. Institutions, Institutional Change and Economic Performance.

6. For more specifics on potential for Dutch cooperatives with partners in the food chain, see chapter on Professor Hughes.

PROFESSOR DAVID HUGHES

Professor David Hughes has held the Sainsbury chair of Management and Agribusiness at Wye College, University of London, since 1991. He has more than 25 years experience in the food industry, both in academic posts and as a co-owner and manager of food companies.

Professor Hughes has a Master of Science and a Doctor of Philosophy degrees relating to marketing of farm production and processed foods that were earned at the University of Newcastle-upon-Tyne. He received his Bachelor of Science degree in agricultural economics at Reading University in England.

Since 1973, Professor Hughes has served on several leading advisory councils for the Canadian government, international institutions, and several business, government, financial and trade associations throughout the world. In this work he has emphasized the formation and evaluation of marketing strategies and concepts.

He and a partner started a successful enterprise, Herbonics Inc., at Homestead, Florida, in 1987. It supplies branded herb products to two of the largest American supermarket chains. In addition, the London professor is also part owner of a venture capital investment firm working in the Washington, D.C.-Baltimore, Maryland area.

A NEW LOOK AT COUNTERVAILING POWER:

Consumers offer new opportunities for farmers and their cooperatives. By Lee Egerstrom

"Let me show you," said Professor David Hughes as he leaped from his comfortable lounge chair at the historic Farmers Club in London.

With pantomime and gestures, voice inflections and shouts, the food marketing expert acted out a scene repeated nightly in supermarkets throughout Europe, North America and East Asia. He portrayed a harried shopper, with young child in tow, stopping to buy groceries enroute home after at day at the office or factory. His head jerked back and forth as the "shopper" studied prices and ordered food in one direction, then demanded the child be quiet with a turn of the head.

Professor Hughes had an appreciative audience. Shouting, and slapping the side of his leg for shock effect to quell the imaginary child, he simulated supermarket chaos that provided a stark contrast to the atmosphere of the club. The 5 o'clock forage for foodstuffs is no match for the decorum of the Farmers Club, where briefcases in the dining room are considered gauche and proper attire is prescribed, down to types of footwear.

Consumers in the industrialized world and technology are tipping the world food system on its head, insists the economist.(1) These changes have "significant implications" for farmers, he adds, as well as offering new opportunities for farmers and their cooperatives who are willing to adjust to consumer-driven markets.(2)

There is debate in the United Kingdom over whether consumers or retailers are forcing change on the food system, he said. "I believe they are consumer- driven." (3) As a result, he said, farmers must shift from being production-oriented to being product-oriented; seeing themselves as suppliers of consumer products in an integrated world food system.

Working back from the supermarket shopper – the final consumer – to the farmer, Professor Hughes sees the following changes occurring to the European and world food systems:

The Consumers

Of all the food consumed in Europe, one-third is consumed away from home in restaurants, snack shops, schools, office and factory cafeterias, and hospitals. The percentage of food consumed away from home is even greater in the United States. This trend toward greater food consumption away from home will continue, he predicts.

Consumers are also changing their diets, he says. While health concerns are well documented causes for changing diets, demographic trends and internationalization of foods are having dramatic impacts on consumer buying. The days are past, he says, when the British homemaker would serve "a meat and two 'vegs' at every meal." Similarly, he jokes, the Dutch have learned there is more to eating than "split-pea soup."

Population growth in Northern Europe is largely from immigration. The immigrants bring new demands for foods to the supermarkets, and retailers are responding to these consumer demands. "Look at the Indonesian influence on Dutch eating habits," he says. Considering these influences on Northern cuisine, Hughes adds, "I say, 'Keep on coming!'"

Equally important, he says, is the impact of international trade and liberalizing food trade within the European Union.

Northern European consumers want fresh fruits and vegetables the year around, not just when they are in season from nearby farms in the northern growing zones. This internationalization of cuisine changes the mix of food products that consumers want in their supermarkets.

"Northern Europeans are adapting to a more Mediterranean diet. The Mediterraneans are eating more Northern European foods. Right now, the Northern Europeans are adapting faster," he says.

The biggest change in consumer buying habits, however, is driven by consumer desire for convenience, Professor Hughes says. The harried homemaker, whom he characterized earlier in acting out the supermarket scene, wants to get home from work, wants to get the child home, and wants to get dinner prepared quickly.

This catering to the tensions of modern society, and meeting needs and wants of two-income families, single-parent families and people living alone – all modern trends documented by Hughes and his colleagues from Wye College, University of London, in the book *Breaking With Tradition* – will continue to bring consumer-driven change to food systems, he says.

For example, the layout of modern supermarkets suggests more changes are forthcoming. Hughes doesn't predict what the changes may be. What he sees as incompatible for consumers in current supermarket arrangements is the compartmentalizing of food groups by fresh produce, refrigerated foods, frozen foods and condiments. The frazzled 5 o'clock shopper is looking for foods in terms of courses that she or he may quickly serve after returning home.

"Consumers have meal solving problems. Part of the meal is to put a dessert on the table. The children want a dessert. Well, fruit can be a dessert. There are frozen desserts. There are canned goods that would make a dessert.

"Can you imagine a (restaurant) menu where desserts are found on pages 2, 4, 7 and 14?"

The Retailers

Even though retailers may be sending shoppers on scavenger hunts for dessert items, the retailers are offering their customers an unprecedented selection of products. This comes with increasing concentration among food retailing firms in most of the industrialized countries, and an increasing concentration of food manufacturing firms that supply branded products to the international retail food industry.

In his published works on retail concentration, Professor Hughes has noted the trend is a Europe-wide phenomenon, granting huge retail companies enormous buying power. As will be discussed later, Hughes isn't certain how retailers use that buying power since there is strong evidence that retailers respond to consumer demands and their own competition at the retail level. Regardless, he has noted that the large retail firms tend to be multinational.(4) Of the top 10 food retailing firms, the five largest are German and French companies; only J Sainsbury plc. in the United Kingdom makes the top 10 list despite large holdings in American retail companies; and combined, the European-based food retailing firms now own about 20 percent of the supermarkets found in the United States.

The retail firms aren't through with expansions and efforts to solidify their food merchandising base, he notes. Western retailers have been rushing into Eastern Europe with the food manufacturers. "They are all nibbling at the Eastern Europe market," he says.

Despite this growth into powerful retail business entities, Hughes sees the retail food industry rapidly changing to cope with pressures from competition and the changing world food system. All current retail trends carry threats and opportunities for farmers and their marketing organizations, he says.

In essentially two decades time, the retail firms first became highly-concentrated national firms and progressed to being trans-national companies. More recently, they've been expanding internationally through joint venture business relations with partner companies and through foreign acquisitions. Now, the spread of their international power is coming through newly created pan-European buying groups.(5)

Hughes and Derek Ray, lecturer in Agricultural and Food Marketing at Wye College, describe the new buying groups as combines seeking to strengthen their companies' buying power while searching for additional product sourcing opportunities. They identify major examples of these buying groups as Eurogroupe, Di-Fra, Buying International Gedelfi

Spar, Deurobuying, European Marketing Distribution and Independent Distributors Association.(6)

While these trends in retailing all represent concentrations of power, they clearly raise questions about how farmers and their cooperatives should position themselves to sell to these large, but few, buying groups. Before attempting to answer those questions, however, farmers should look at the buying groups' second objective spelled out in the Hughes-Ray definition. That is, to broaden the member-retailers' product sourcing opportunities.

New players are being brought into the integrated world food system despite the retail concentration. Retailers are driven to look for new products and sources of supply to give them market advantages over competitors, Hughes says. Moreover, he notes, the biggest increase in European and North American new food product introductions are coming from specially made store brands, or private label, products ordered by the retail firms themselves. This trend opens international trade opportunities for farmers' cooperatives and small food manufacturers alike.

Food Servers and Food Manufacturers

The fastest growing segment of the food industry is foodservice, Hughes says. These providers of convenient foods that are served in restaurants and institutional feeding programs are riding a growing market even though the entire food industry is considered "mature," or even stagnant in most developed countries.

Eating meals away from home is gaining speed in affluent societies, he says. Now, he adds, the trends are circling back and food manufacturers and retailers are starting to offer consumers more choices of chilled, ready-to-eat foods that require minimal heating or preparation at home.

This is a logical extension of the "eating out" trend, he said. "I call it eating out-in," he said.

The British call this new, prepared foods market "chilled foods." "It is not the so-called TV dinners," Hughes insists. It can be restaurant-quality prepared foods to simplify the menu solving problems for the harried office or factory worker he characterized earlier. Or it can be exquisite, exotic fare from other regions and cultures of the world, sating the consumer's appetite for international cuisine even when the homemaker or hobby chef has neither the time nor the knowledge to prepare the food.

Marks & Spencer is the largest purveyor of chilled foods in the UK, he says. "You can stop after work and pick up Chinese dim sum (appetizers), chicken chow mein and a bottle of Romanian wine to serve three (people) for 10 pounds. It would cost you 35 pounds in the restaurant."

The impact on the food industry is starting to be felt. A conference for the European food industry was held in 1992 to probe whether chilled foods were leading to "confrontation or cooperation" between retailers and food service companies. (7)

Some companies are choosing to confront. Retailers with large stores and space capabilities may prepare these foods internally, thus raising the value of the food ingredients they sell. Other firms will turn to industrial kitchens operated by food service companies for these value-added services. When this occurs, more strategic partnerships are formed.

The large, multinational food manufacturing firms are striking similar arrangements, Professor Hughes observes. General Mills, the No. 2 American breakfast cereal maker and large marketer of home baking products and snack foods, teamed up with Switzerland's Nestle in 1989 to promote its breakfast cereals in Europe. Cereal Partners Worldwide, their joint venture based in Switzerland, now combines General Mills's extensive cereal product line with Nestle's leading marketing and distribution skills throughout Europe.

In the interim, the Hughes-Ray study of horizontal alliances, cited above, chronicles Nestle forming a similar arrangement with Coca-Cola (USA) in 1990 to develop ready-to-drink coffee and tea drinks outside of Japan; PepsiCo (USA) teamed with Unilever, the Dutch-British food giant, in 1991 to develop new markets and new drink products for Unilever's Lipton brand teas; PepsiCo and General Mills merged their European snack food businesses in 1992 into a Holland-based joint venture, Snack Partners Worldwide; and Unilever formed a joint venture with BSN (France) in 1993 to market ice cream and yogurt products worldwide. (8)

Standing alone, all of these companies represent marketing power not yet achieved by farmer-owned cooperatives in any nation. Combined in strategic partnerships, they represent annual turnover and marketing power that exceed anything found in the world's equally concentrated automobile manufacturing industry. (9)

This combined strength notwithstanding, the impact of these relationships may not be evident yet at most European farms. The same cannot be said at Europe's food wholesale firms.

The Wholesalers

"The role of the wholesaler is being squeezed out," says Professor Hughes. They become the odd-man out, he explains, as retailers want Just-In-Time deliveries (a distribution management system), food service companies create their own distribution systems – partly in response to the perishable nature of their products, and the large food manufacturing companies specialize in marketing and distribution.

Researchers at Strathclyde University have completed a study that asked if wholesalers can survive in the United Kingdom, Hughes said. The Strathclyde conclusion was that wholesaling will remain a function of the UK food system, but not at present levels. Increasingly, he said, food retailers and food manufacturing companies are employing third-party transportation firms and lorry operators to make deliveries while their own marketing staffs take over product marketing functions from wholesalers.

Hughes says population density in countries, such as the Benelux nations, and historical food system differences will play out differently across Europe. But the take over of wholesaling functions by food companies and retailers, and the farming out of distribution to third-party firms, will continue, he predicts. "We're going to see more of that."

The Farmers

All of these changes in the structure of the world food system will affect the farm and farmer-owned cooperatives, Hughes says. How it does depends on the type of food production the farmers and cooperatives represent, and how willing they are to change in step with other sectors of the industry to seize opportunities.

At the wholesale level, he notes, farmers stand to lose the price discovery functions formerly provided by wholesalers who brought farmers and retailers together. This raises serious questions for the cooperative auction systems in the Netherlands, he adds, even though he is aware Dutch cooperatives are exploring ways to supply large retail stores with vegetables and cut flowers under long-term contracts consistent with retailers' direct buying trends.

Cooperatives, too, can strike strategic alliance and partnership arrangements with firms that have different expertise. Usually, that will mean finding a marketing partner the same way General Mills is bringing its breakfast cereals to Europe through the marketing and logistics of Nestle. "I don't see how smaller firms can go it alone," he said. "To serve the accounts, you've got to be large."

That does open opportunities for farmers and their cooperatives, he concludes. Pooled, the farmers have both volume and economies of scale to supply large retail accounts or to form partnerships with other firms that can assist marketing and add value to farm commodities.

"I've been telling farmers in a strawberry cooperative they shouldn't undersell themselves," Hughes said. That British cooperative has 40 percent of the UK's strawberry market during June and July. "That means the farmers have clout." And it also means that the cooperative is in position to be the principal supplier of strawberries 12 months a year to large retail firm customers, whether the British farmers grow the strawberries or import them out of season.

The potato industry offers another example of how farmers and cooperatives can be important players in the evolving world food system, he says. Ten years ago, there were about two types of potatoes sold in retail stores, and critics of the food industry were worrying the concentration of food companies was dangerous for bio-diversity. Now, he notes, there are from 10 to 12 potato items in supermarkets each day that are made from different potatoes bred from different seed stocks.

The same special breeding for niche markets is occurring to large field crops such as the classes of wheats and types of corn, he adds. This fragmentation of the food industry should also open doors for cooperatives.

The most important change in future business strategies for cooperatives, however, is to recognize they make consumer products – like the big brand name companies – whether they are dealing with raw materials or finished products. "Consumers will determine who succeeds," he says.

For too long, he adds, farmers and cooperatives have been production oriented and not aware of consumer wants and needs. He cites the New Zealand lamb industry as a classic example. The New Zealanders have worked at being the world's low-cost producers and then try to ship frozen legs of lamb to markets around the world. That harried shopper –

depicted back at the Farmers Club in London – doesn't want a frozen leg of lamb to serve a family of three immediately after work, he said.

Chapter Footnotes

1. Hughes, David (ed.). Breaking With Tradition: Building Partnerships & Alliances in the European Food Industry. Wye College Press, London. 1994.

2. Hughes, David. "Change Brings Opportunity – Go For It!" Winning essay, Royal Agricultural Society of England first annual essay competition. 1995.

3. Hughes made the point emphatically at the beginning of an interview for this book.

4. Hughes. "Change Brings Opportunity – Go For It!."

5. Hughes, David and Ray, Derek. "Types of Partnerships & Alliances in the European Food Industry." (Chapter 3.) Breaking With Tradition.

6. Ibid.

7. Ibid.

8. Ibid.

9. The writer's observation from comparing gross worldwide revenues.

LEE EGERSTROM

Lee Egerstrom, 53, is the agribusiness and trade writer for the St. Paul *Pioneer Press* newspaper in Minnesota, in the north-central region of the United States. He is author of <u>Make No Small Plans: A Cooperative Revival for Rural America</u>, a 1995 book that explains New Generation Cooperatives as a tool for farmers to create local processing and manufacturing cooperatives to raise farm incomes and support community development.

Egerstrom is a former Washington correspondent for Knight-Ridder Newspapers, a past president of the National Association of Agricultural Journalists and was an officer of the National Press Club in Washington, D.C. He is also a member of the Society of American Business Editors and Writers. Egerstrom has served on the national board for the Commission on Church and Society, the social services and hunger program arm of the Evangelical Lutheran Church in America. He began studying Dutch and European cooperatives in 1985 while on a sabbatical program sponsored by the Stichting Atlantic-Pacific Exchange Programme based at Rotterdam.

Egerstrom has also written *Rediscovering Cooperation*, a study published by the Minnesota Association of Cooperatives, and *Newspaper Farm Editors in a Changing World*, a study on agricultural journalism at American newspapers. His professional awards include the National Press Club's Washington Correspondents Award for Congressional Reporting (1980), the Newspaper Farm Editor of the Year Award from the National Association of Agricultural Journalists (1985), and in 1992, he received the J.S. Russell Memorial Award, the highest honor bestowed by the agricultural journalists for career contributions to agricultural journalism.

NEEDED: A COURSE CORRECTION IN AGRICULTURE:

Horizontal expansion is disastrous for rural life.
By Lee Egerstrom

Dr. Theo Schut, the Dutch economist and economic development director for the Brabant region around Eindhoven, likes to point out a slight omission in the Bible. Genesis tells how God made the heavens and the earth before resting on the seventh day. In the second week, according to Schut, Dutch farmers and engineers rolled up their sleeves and set about building polders.

Well, maybe his timeline isn't right. But he's not far off. From the earliest times, all of human society has been changing, and changing its landscapes. Agriculture, transportation and institutions have been reshaped to accommodate larger human populations. Most of this change was along a horizontal plane in agriculture as technology allowed farmers to cultivate larger parcels of land and care for larger flocks and herds. Trade, and the institutions that support trade, also developed and adapted technologies to facilitate horizontal expansion of agriculture to new, distant lands and countries. This is the economic history of the New World where land for horizontal expansion could be found – through various means – in the Americas, Australia, New Zealand and, for a time, in Africa. It is also the economic history of Europe where people, such as the Dutch, discovered it was less costly to develop trade and shipping than to reclaim the North Sea and keep building polders.

Change is constant. At the present time, it is coming to world agriculture with dramatic speed. There is little time for gradual, evolutionary adjustments. Markets, which can be personalized to mean consumers, will not wait for farmers who are slow of foot. An integrated world food system has emerged that is now rationing informal "quota" rights that determine who can produce what crops and raise what livestock, who can process the raw materials, who can further process products for the consumers' supermarkets and tables, who can market and distribute the food products, and, ultimately, who receives which portions of the consumers' food spending.(1)

This is the global environment that inspired this book. It is an environment that requires farmers, cooperative managers, economists and social scientists to look vertically as well as horizontally to explore issues of economic justice, environmental responsibility, and social goals of economic development. This must be done while weighing those issues against basic, capitalistic economic opportunities. Reasoning together, farmers and their cooperative colleagues in management must deduce where they can stake a claim to parts of the integrated world food system, and where they have little power and must merely take what the system offers them.

This book, then, offers contemporary views of leading economists, food industry experts and trade observers from around the world who examine the forces now converging on agriculture and the global food system. As one of the book's three editors, I know the content of the other chapters. It is from this vantage point only that I forego any sense of humility and place this essay before the following chapters, as explained in the Introduction to the English language edition.

"Good times" and "bad times"

In 30 years of journalism, I've written about the constant cycles of "farm crises" that have swept through the American Middle West, the subsequent number of economic recoveries, and the occasional "boom cycles" as well. Over time, the so-called "good times" become more controversial and may inflict more damage to the rural economy and rural life than the so-called "bad times."

The consequences of these cycles are different in North America than in Northern Europe. Farmers in the United States and Canada, in general, have been more trade oriented in recent decades and have been more content to produce commodities for world markets. Denmark's pig industry and Holland's horticulture are contradictions to this generalization. But also, in general, Northern Europeans have more highly developed cooperative enterprises than are found in North America. These institutions generate more income for producer-members from processing, reducing farm dependence on world commodity markets.(2) The role played by cooperatives in Northern Europe helps stabilize the swings in world agriculture cycles while American and Canadian farmers remain free to reap greater benefits during years of boom and suffer greater losses during bust cycles.

Hard times are easy for the general public to understand. There is public support for farmers during such moments. It often exceeds the public support provided idle auto workers and other people during hard times for various industries. That support comes from the agrarian culture and history of the United States, just as similar responses in Europe are social products from historical memory.

Less easy to understand is the harmful side effects caused by boom cycles in agriculture. Because American and Canadian farmers have become so export oriented, strong exports and rising grain prices trigger rapid expansions in land holdings as farmers buy their neighbors' land and expand horizontally. This horizontal expansion of agriculture is extremely destructive to the broader rural economy.

Consequences of horizontal expansion

The number of hectares (acres) under cultivation or the size of livestock herds and flocks doesn't support economic activity in rural communities. The number of rural families – rural population – provides the lifeblood of local economies. Thus, rural America and rural Canada face a predicament in which the new, integrated world food system may be financially rewarding for surviving farm operators while at the same time it contributes to weaker rural communities and an increase in rural poverty.(3)

Even though similar forces are undoubtedly at work in the more densely populated countries in Europe, the impact may not be as great on European rural communities. When farm land is broken loose from farmsteads and taken over by expanding farmers, rural homes are likely to become homes for families that choose to live in the country and commute to jobs in nearby cities. The touring motorist isn't likely to notice the restructuring occurring in the countryside. The rural merchant isn't likely to notice much difference in local business activity, either.

Such changes in rural population are also occurring within the 100-kilometer radius of North American cities. Out on the prairie, however, the future existence of towns is threatened. Whole communities will disappear because they fail to serve a modern social or economic function, just as my great-grandparents' home town in Sweden cannot be found on modern maps. I've written about the death of a more contemporary town in western Minnesota:

Georgeville Is Dead

"GEORGEVILLE – The last indignity will be when the Minnesota Highway Department stops putting Georgeville on the map. That may be soon. There's no one left to be offended.

"Georgeville has completed the metamorphosis that threatens the assets of many rural Minnesotans and the continued existence of dozens of rural towns, many of them much larger than Georgeville....

"People once had faith in Georgeville. The general store once served as a country shopping center. Upstairs, there were rooms for rent; and it housed a grocery, a land office, a beauty parlor and a corner gas station. At one time it had an office for a bank.

"Residents remaining in the area remember the store in more recent times as a headquarters for a 'hippie' colony that tried to revive Georgeville. The building still stands tall, but its pink and lavender facade reminds the natives nearby of those last occupants.

"As the colony packed up and moved out of town, one of the members took spray paint in hand and left a biblical epitaph on the store's north wall: "And the prophet said, 'Your old men shall dream dreams, and your young men shall see visions, and where there is no vision, the people perish'." **(4)**

At the time, I thought the threat of ghost towns was only a problem for rural areas of America, Canada, Australia, New Zealand, Brazil and Argentina. Perhaps it could happen on Denmark's lesser populated islands, or remote areas of Norway or Finland. But not in most areas on continental Europe.

I was wrong.

On a visit to Germany in August, 1995, a friend greeted me and jokingly said he knew why I had come. "Rural America is dying," he said. "I just read about it in the newspaper."

He had. A leading German newspaper had published an article about the small town of America, Germany.**(5)** The town was situated along the former border between East and West Germany. Given that location, it hadn't attracted industrial investments. As border barriers came down, farms began expanding from both the East and West side. Now, my host said, the town appeared to be standing in the way of agricultural expansion with no apparent economic reason to survive as a municipality.**(6)**

The problem was familiar. I might add that Heidelburg and New Munch, in rural Minnesota, and Berlin, North Dakota, don't inspire great confidence in the future of America's rural America. The same can be said about Midwestern American towns named Stockholm, Oslo, Vienna, Paris, Rome, Cairo, Alexandria, Athens, Ghent and New London.

Pressures to expand horizontally

Horizontal expansion of agriculture is inevitable when technology changes economies of scale, and when international trade markets reward well-capitalized users of technology. Pressure for horizontal expansion of farm units will continue throughout Europe in response to European Union integration and from more liberalized world markets in general. This is inevitable, and, I would argue, desirable: I'm not aware of any attempt to legislate against technology or markets, and thus repeal 'laws' of economics, that didn't create more problems than it solved.

The results of this expansion shouldn't be as dramatic in Europe as they are in some parts of the more sparsely populated states and provinces of North America. Industrial expansion and commuters will fill in behind exiting farmers and agricultural workers. But it is a threat to the agrarian rural community structure still found throughout much of Europe.

This book testifies to the fact that some farmers, cooperative business leaders and academics are exploring ways to change economies of scale in Western Europe and North America. A similar exercise – an even larger one – is desperately needed to assess agricultural development in South America, Africa, and emerging areas of Asia and Eastern Europe. It seems apparent that international institutions, such as United Nations agencies, the World Bank and regional development banks, will need to be part of this task.

Technology transfer and all things associated with open borders and freer trade carry the risk of holding back rural economic progress for people living in rural areas in many regions of the world. It leads to more horizontal expansion of agriculture. Manorialism and plantation agriculture still are problems for rural people who do not profit beyond a subsistence standard of living in many rural areas. Their problems are similar to those of Northern Europeans in the 18th and early 19th Centuries. Today, management of "crown properties," or "church holdings," or former communist farm properties of more recent times, is made easier with 21st Century technology. It makes little difference that

44

the new landed nobility is an agribusiness company, a group of foreign investors, an existing landed gentry or wealthy, expanding farmers. (7)

Looking up: New Generation Cooperatives

There are rural communities in North America that serve as models for researchers and visitors from around the world. These communities are pooling resources and building what Americans now call "New Generation Cooperatives." They are trying to make adjustments in economies of scale from the ground up, using value-added processing and product manufacturing for its members to derive more of their incomes from the consumers instead of world commodity markets. In short, they are finding a new approach to many of the objectives being carried out by the large Dutch and Danish cooperatives, and the French farmers' cooperatives in Brittany; but they are attacking the market from the opposite direction.

New Generation Cooperatives will be explored in more detail in a following chapter. (8) These new businesses attempt to add value locally – within their own community – to the members' grains, vegetables, fruits and animals. It may involve a group of farmers in an area building modern pig barns and using their grains as feed in a large livestock enterprise. It can mean a relatively small group of farmers – mostly of a young age – pooling resources to build large dairy barns they jointly operate, or to grow organic food crops for niche markets. It can mean similar investments in chickens and eggs production, beef cattle feedlots, or bison raising on prairie ranches and Indian reservations in the Dakotas.

The new cooperatives also appeal to small groups of blueberry farmers in the northwoods of Wisconsin, Saskatoon berry farmers in Canada's Saskatchewan province, whose unusual wild berries are like a mixture of blueberries and Scandinavia's cloud berries. They are especially helpful for small, specialty crops farmers in the Pacific Northwest states of Washington and Oregon, who combine small-scale food production with forestry enterprises.

After meeting initial organization and marketing objectives, these New Generation Cooperatives soon prompt members to pool more resources to do value-added work beyond marketing and procuring supplies. Processing and packaging fruit preserves is an examples, and making regional wines is another. The farmers at Renville, Minnesota, have progressed in three years time from building cooperatively-owned barns for laying hens to building a processing plant that cracks the eggs and separates egg whites from egg yolks. Liquid egg components are then shipped to food industry companies under long-term supply contracts that assure better incomes and profits for the cooperative's 140 members than they could realize by individually selling their grains, chickens and eggs to the U.S. commodity markets.

How does this differ from existing, traditional cooperatives in the United States, or from the successful cooperatives in Europe? Professor Cook will explain some of these objectives in a later chapter. The key difference, however, is one of strategy. Traditional cooperatives were formed for defensive purposes as farmers sought protection from perceived failures in marketing. The new generation cooperative is strictly an offensive response to markets; farmers join the new entities with the goal of returning more of the consumers' food outlay to their farms and communities than can be derived from basic commodity production.

"Eureka": We've found models

As following chapters will show, strategies can and do change over time. The successful and large cooperatives today have changed and employ different strategies, both to better serve customers – as Hughes explains – and to better serve members.

The colorful history of the potato farmers who started the Avebe cooperative in the northern Netherlands offers a classic example of pooling resources for defensive purposes, then progressing to an offensive strategy. Avebe started in response to private potato factories that banded together as an informal buying cooperative under the name Eureka and were thus able to dictate potato prices. The farmers fought back, buying and taking over the factories. (9)

Americans who know Avebe's history enjoy it. The exclamation, "Eureka! We have found it!" spread word across America of the gold discovery that started the California Gold Rush of 1849. Over the years, northern Dutch farmers and their colleagues across the border in Germany have discovered gold in their potatoes, too. Their enhanced farm income benefits from potatoes began after Avebe moved from the defensive to the offensive and began developing hundreds of industrial and pharmaceutical products from potato starch.

In the United States, cooperatives followed a similar path from defensive to offensive strategies but have not gained comparable dominance in supplying farm needs or marketing farm commodities. The greatest number of farmer-owned cooperatives were started in the old Northwest frontier states which includes most of the territory west and north of Chicago. It wasn't accidental development.

The Northwest territory was a late American frontier. Waves of immigrants came to the region from Germany, the Scandinavian countries, the Netherlands, Belgium, France, Ireland and Great Britain. These settlers helped establish farm supply and marketing cooperatives for defensive reasons – they wanted to get supplies and household goods out to the frontier; and they wanted a voice in marketing the grains and animals they produced. They created cooperatives similar to those their ancestors had started or their cousins were then starting in Northern Europe. They created institutions and localized political parties that continue to bear closer resemblance to social movements and parties found in Europe than to national parties and social institutions found in other regions of America.

Land O'Lakes is now a diversified dairy cooperative and dairy foods company. It does look like an American cousin of Campina Melkunie, although less diverse in its operations. Harvest States Cooperatives and Farmland Industries, American giants in farm supply and marketing, are rapidly expanding into value-added areas of food processing, pig production, flour milling, and vegetable oil manufacturing. Along with other regional American marketing cooperatives, they are partners with various European cooperatives in owning the A.C. Toepfer International marketing company at Hamburg, Germany.

As the English-language edition of this book was going to press, Harvest States Cooperatives was preparing to change its constitutional by-laws at an annual meeting to give the cooperative greater flexibility in forming subsidiaries, joint ventures and strategic alliances with local cooperatives. In many regards, Harvest States Cooperatives was transforming itself into a "holding company" cooperative along the lines advocated by Professor Grosskopf and others in later chapters.

Cenex, the large farm supply and petroleum cooperative, is another American cooperative that deserves watching by other cooperatives throughout the world. To use a term popular with today's industries everywhere, Cenex is constantly "re-engineering" itself.

This firm started out as Farmers Union Central Exchange to buy farm supplies cooperatively. It is owned by more than 1,000 community-based farm supply and petroleum cooperatives. Like the new generation co-ops starting new ventures, the local Cenex co-ops keep finding new community services and value-added activities to offer their members and towns. In turn, Cenex must constantly change the mix of products and services it supplies member cooperatives. For instance, the local cooperatives have now made Cenex the fastest growing chain of "convenience stores" in the United States as petroleum service stations expand to include small grocery stores and entertainment (video) rental shops.

Every day, it seems, models for cooperative action and community development spring forth from new cooperative businesses and from existing cooperatives that are renewing themselves.

Among the more interesting new cooperative ventures now influencing rural America is the Bison Cooperative at New Rockford, North Dakota, where ranchers are returning to raising "buffalo," or North American bison, instead of beef cattle breeds. The bison meat returns four times the amount of farm revenue that could be gained from beef, per animal, and the ranchers also earn money from the slaughtering and marketing performed at their own slaughter plant.

A similar new venture is an ostrich and emu cooperative formed in rural areas west of Minneapolis, Minnesota, where urban sprawl is making land too costly to grow most farm crops. New cooperatives in Wisconsin and southeastern Minnesota are also saving access to the dairy industry for Amish farm families. The Amish are members of old European religious groups that don't use electricity and modern conveniences; thus, their unrefrigerated milk cannot be sold except for manufacturing purposes under U.S. health regulations.

Seizing countervailing power

All of these moves by farmers and their cooperatives are responses to changing world and domestic market forces and institutional changes. Whether starting from the bottom up, as they are in the United States, or from the top down, as is more often the case in Europe, the motivation is the same. It is the quest for countervailing power, as identified and described by the Canadian-American economist John Kenneth Galbraith. (10)

What may be forgotten with time, however, is that Professor Galbraith spent a great amount of his attention on government policy as a provider of countervailing power for farmers and other business entrepreneurs engaged in open and democratic markets. The Harvard University economist strongly argued that farmers would have an easier time acquiring countervailing power if the food industry was more controlled by monopolistic or oligopolistic powers. This argument, in turn, has given intellectual justification for governmental farm programs throughout the industrialized world.(11) But as others in this book discuss, concentration at higher rungs of the food ladder is increasing even as government support for agriculture is declining.

Some of the economists profiled in this book examine how these relationships have changed. Professor Ruttan, for one, says these changes put pressure on farm policies such as the United States' price support programs and Europe's Common Agriculture Policy. Without doubt, the retreat from past farm price protection and trade protection now underway is changing whatever countervailing power cooperatives may have enjoyed in the past.

Where do modern farmers find countervailing power in the absence of government "safety nets" ? Put another way, where do farmers turn to increase farm revenues and family incomes?

The American experience suggests that farmers cannot gain market power through horizontal expansion of agriculture without imposing high social costs on their nation and communities during periods of adjustment. This expansion displaces people and rural jobs, leaving weakened or dying towns and more rural poverty. Employment rates show growth in industrial/manufacturing jobs is not keeping pace with population, and jobs in agriculture are declining.(12)

A vertical expansion of agriculture through cooperative models, however, holds promise of offering farmers and their families a bright future. It can also create jobs within the farmers' own communities..

From top to bottom, the world food system is being reshaped, redefined and reallocated to new players. It is happening throughout the Eastern world with the collapse of communism and economic reforms in China. And, we have been recently reminded, it is happening among Western cooperatives and regional institutions as well:

A provincial governor from Russia visited North Dakota in early 1995 to study New Generation Cooperatives. Unbeknownst to the Russian official or his escorts from the U.S. State Department, the hot debate topic in North Dakota was whether to sell the state-owned North Dakota Mill and Elevator, an enterprise left over from the state's socialist days in the early 1900s. After his initial shock and disbelief were put to rest, the visiting dignitary volunteered, "Ladies and gentlemen, if you need help with privatization, perhaps we Russians can be of assistance. "(**13**)

Yes, we must all learn from each other.

There is an urgency for planning and decision making if farmers are to stake out claims to be part of the new world markets. All past history suggests that markets do fill voids. What farmers fail to do now will leave windows of opportunity for others in the food chain. For the present, the emerging world food market still offers an opportunity for farmers seeking countervailing power.

Chapter Footnotes

1. This was the central theme of a published paper calling on American cooperatives to increase their role in value-added processing and consumer food manufacturing. Egerstrom, Lee. *Rediscovering Cooperation.* (Minnesota Association of Cooperatives, 1994.)

2. For a more detailed look at American cooperatives, see the chapter on Professor Michael Cook.

3. Egerstrom, Lee. Make No Small Plans: A Cooperative Revival for Rural America. (Lone Oak Press, 1995.)

4. St. Paul *Pioneer Press.* Jan. 21, 1985.

5. I do not read German and I don't have the Berlin newspaper article mentioned. However, agricultural economists at Humboldt University in Berlin discussed it at some length, for my benefit, commenting on both the importance of the news story and its clever writing.

6. This interpretation was offered by Professor Dr. Harald von Witzke, Humboldt University at Berlin.

7. Participants from parts of Asia and Central America gave considerable attention to the displacement of people from the land and ways in which cooperatives can foster rural economic development at a June, 1995, conference in Saskatoon, Saskatchewan. The cooperative conference was sponsored by the province of Saskatchewan, Canadian cooperatives and the University of Saskatchewan.

8. See: Cook.

9. From centennial history book of Avebe, Veendam, Netherlands.

10. Galbraith, John Kenneth. American Capitalism: The Concept of Countervailing Power. (Houghton Mifflin Co., 1952.)

11. The writer's interpretation of Galbraith's comments.

12. Hamrick, Karen S. <u>Agricultural Outlook</u>. (Economic Research Service, U.S. Department of Agriculture. June 1996.)

13. As retold by North Dakota Agriculture Commissioner Sara Vogel, who led efforts to retain state ownership of the historic mill and elevator company.

PART TWO: ASSESSING COOPERATIVE STRENGTHS WHEN APPROACHING CHANGE

PROFESSOR DR. ROEL JAAP IN 'T VELD

Professor Dr. Roel Jaap in 't Veld studied Dutch law at Leiden University where he gained his undergraduate degree in 1964. He received his doctorate there in 1975. In 1977, after holding a number of positions at Leiden University, he was appointed ordinary professor in Public Administration at the University of Nijmegen.

In 1979, Professor in 't Veld became chairman of a national committee appointed to develop methods for the assessment of science policy in the Netherlands. Thereafter, in 1982, In 't Veld was appointed Director-General of the Higher Education and Scientific Research Board of the Ministry of Education and Science. Subsequently, he became ordinary professor in Public Administration at Erasmus University, Rotterdam, and since 1990 he has held a similar position at Leiden University.

For a period of time in 1993, Professor in 't Veld was State Secretary of the Ministry of Education and Science. He also held the positions of chairman of the Supervisory Council for the Information Management Group, Groningen; Rector of the Foundation for the Intervarsity Studies on Organizational Theory and professor of the endowed chair of Organizational Theory at the University of Amsterdam. Since 1995, he has also served as Dean of the Utrecht School of Postgraduate Continuing Education at the Utrecht State University.

Professor in 't Veld holds several additional positions outside his full-time education post, and he is the author of a large number of publications and books.

SOCIETY AND THE FORCES FOR CHANGE

Cooperatives as an organizational form for the future

By Professor Gert van Dijk and Pieter Bos

Not many managers of cooperative businesses are willing to openly discuss their personal values and business standards, says Professor Roel in 't Veld, a leading Dutch observer of organizational and institutional behavior. "They are afraid of being branded 'true believers'," zealots, or protagonists of the cooperative structure as a third alternative between liberal, laissez faire capitalism on one hand and socialism on the other.(1)

Roel in 't Veld, professor of the chair of Public Administration at Erasmus University in Rotterdam, says values cannot be isolated from a cooperative business. "... Collective values are the foundation of the cooperative as a form of collaboration amongst members, even though these values are influenced by both shifts in social values and economic developments to which cooperative firms are exposed," he says.

At a time when cooperatives are growing in size and scope, values may need to be re-examined. Values may be sensitive to increases in scale, or size, in the organization, and there may be a scale, or level, at which point fundamental values are at risk of crumbling away.

These questions may not be receiving adequate academic or institutional attention where businesses are viewed as a business form or legal entity, he says. "I am not in a position to judge that," he explains. "However, I do think that the social sciences are able to pass judgment on the cooperative as a form of collaboration."

Professor in 't Veld, who is one of Holland's most respected experts on public administration, looks at the collaboration aspect of cooperative businesses and weighs that against groups, or sects, that farm or work together.(2) The two are polar opposites, he insists, even though both rely on collaboration amongst their members. "Its difference from the cooperative lies in the sect's ascribing a moral value to everything. A cooperative limits its activities to the economic dimension. The cooperative and sects do, however, coincide where the fundamental values of their own association are concerned."

To look at the cooperative, as opposed to a sect, one needs to look at the arrangement for collaboration in the firm; or put another way, at its roots. According to In 't Veld, the agreement to collaborate is based on at least three categories of core values. They are integral to the rest of his argument.

"It is related to deflecting or reducing risk (e.g. insurance or less exposure to the caprice of the market); to economic advantage (e.g. promoting a fair return for one's labor through market corrections); and cooperative culture (moderating self-interest, solidarity, the strong helping the weak, etc.). In other words, we are speaking of a community that stands for risk reduction, meritocracy (social status related to ability and achievement), and fairness of income distribution," he says.

Values and scale

What, In 't Veld asks himself, is the relationship between collective values and the collective agreement that binds the cooperative organization? And, he asks, how do developments within the firm, and society in general, affect this relationship?

That may vary from cooperative to cooperative, based on their different businesses, but what fascinates In 't Veld especially is the relationship between values and the firm's scale of operations. "I wonder how critical the relationship is between the two; in other words, is there a point of scale beyond which these typical cooperative values cease to exist? The following example illustrates my point:

"Originally, the cooperative – let's suppose it concerns collective fire insurance – was established against a backdrop of sufficient social control. If anyone cheated the system by setting fire to his farm, everyone else quickly knew about it. Within the closed society of the cooperative, a system of behavioral values grew, (establishing) what was and wasn't done, what was and wasn't allowed, and what was and wasn't tolerated.

"If cheating were to become a regular occurrence, the basis for the cooperative would cease to exist: If you can't trust one another, the transaction costs become so high that it is no longer attractive to continue the relationship.(3) The decision to stop is easily made. Of course, then it is back to the trenches again, to face the risks all on your own.," In 't Veld says.

"But imagine that you enlarge the scale of your activities, and that, in doing so, the enlargement takes place in a period during which social values are in a state of decline and the values of the individual take precedence.(4) This gives rise to an increase in anonymity and a decrease in social control, all at the same time as the moral value of not cheating the system is waning," he says.

When this happens, In 't Veld warns, members begin chipping away at the foundation of their own organization. "There is little to stop you from creating the very situation that you have insured yourself against – for your own profit. The alternative is to keep a check on the creation of risks, but that is a losing battle," he says. "The result is the 'holiday insurance syndrome' (5) whereby many people dishonestly claim damage or lost personal property on their insurance policies. The premiums for 'holiday' insurance continually increase as a consequence. Generally, this sort of agreement will not last for long, I think." (6)

In 't Veld says the above is only one specific example, but it raises a more general issue for cooperatives and their members. What is the relationship between a cooperative's values and the agreement that binds the membership, he asks. And have the critical limits of that relationship been reached?

"I do know that the original values and scale of operations that were the foundation of the (members' business) agreement no longer exist, not even in a committed cooperative," he says. "That is not to say that there is nothing of them left. There is, but everything is different. The scale of operations is different, the values are different and, as a result, so too are the relationships in the cooperative."

Solidarity

How far can a cooperative go? Where is the danger in the relationship between values and the cooperative's business agreement?

That depends largely on the degree of involvement of members in their cooperative, says In 't Veld. He also points out that involvement is something that develops, from the moment the cooperative is founded.

The cooperative's primary goal is the economic benefit of its members through moderating (pooling, combining) their members' interests, he says. "You could call that a modest form of solidarity. That is the basis of the agreement. After a while it appears that the agreement is an economic success, which makes it attractive to farmers who are not members.

"But that's not all," he continues. "In the wake of the economic relationship, other values – ones of a more permanent nature – develop. You could call it 'emotional investment' in the cooperative. You, as a member, might then be prepared to say: 'The cooperative is dear to me. It's more than money – I'm part of it. Through it, I participate in society.' According to the theory of social constructs, people begin to define their perception of reality in these terms, too," he adds.(7)

Professor in 't Veld says cooperatives should look at the conditions that are critical to sustain member involvement, and thus, loyalty, in their companies. Conversely, if membership involvement is decreasing, managers and board members should be pondering when they have reached a danger zone.

This becomes more than a simple matter of values and business scale, In 't Veld says. "Our evolution as an information society is also an important factor in this matter," he says.

In 't Veld says he expects that a growing number of agribusiness firms will reduce their operations to what he calls "transcendental services." Instead of supplying a "concrete," or finished product, the cooperative may instead market the know-how to produce that product. Such a development will likely change the relationship between the cooperative and its members, he says. "Will they (also) become members on a transcendental plane?" This is a question facing all society, he notes. He asks himself what his points of contact will be in the future. "Will my pals be my Internet contacts or will they be the people working on the floor below my office – people whom I have never met and perhaps never will?"

Ultimately, cooperatives – members and managers – must evaluate what separates them from a private or public limited liability company. The difference is related to the set of values maintained within the cooperative, In 't Veld says. It recalls the three crucial values he identified earlier: risk reduction, meritocracy, and fairness of income distribution.

All three can be found in any cooperative, he says, although the emphasis the cooperative places on each will vary from firm to firm. Their presence in the cooperative, however, isn't enough, he emphasizes.

"That combination of values must be expressed in the organizational agreement. **(8)** Specifically, it must be expressed in institutional aspects such as distribution of returns or profit, and levels of contribution to overhead," In 't Veld says. In periods of transition, the challenge will be to retain these values when the cooperative's sphere of influence is changing, when it is reassessing its role as a local, regional or national company, and when the company is trying to distinguish itself from other, competitive companies.

Trust

"But that is not the end of it," Professor in 't Veld says. "The attitude of management will have to support the value of moderation of self-interest. They, too, will have to emulate the attitude of not always wanting only the best out of the bargain. In the end, it is about the influence of all three central values operating within the organization.

"That will promote the mutual trust that is integral to such an approach: 'We can do this because, after all, we're not out to cheat each other'," he says.

Four categories of cooperatives

There are four basic categories of organization, says Professor in 't Veld. Each is a stable organizational form with its own values, standards and culture. Similarly, he says, cooperatives are structured along four categories of organization. He uses a simple matrix to explain the categories.

Nature of Output ╲ Organizational Status	Task-Oriented	Market-Oriented
Product Goals	1	3
Capacity Goals	2	4

(Graphic by Marisa Egerstrom)

First category: A task-oriented organization with product goals. It can be a fairly small, simple organization in which the members actively participate in setting policy, which management is required to implement. Management is task oriented.

Second category: A task-oriented organization with capacity goals. This differs form the previous type in that it no longer decides directly the nature of its end-product nor to whom the product is sold. Often, the cooperative just supplies a broker. This large customer will specify what, and in what quantity, the cooperative is to deliver. It is an organizational form in which a great deal of stress is inherent. Management is caught in the middle, between its large client and the members. It is, he chuckles, "a recipe for trouble."

Third category: A market-oriented organization with product goals. In this form of organization, policy will increasingly be made by management. It will on its own initiative actively seek clients for its products and also maintain direct contact with individual members.

Member meetings are less a forum for policy-making and more a sounding board for ideas and attitudes under this organizational system. In't Veld says this is a stable organizational type if the cooperative has strong markets and products that are good sellers.

Fourth category: A market-oriented organization with capacity goals. In this type of organization, the relationship between the management and the market is crucial, he says. "Members have been relegated to the sidelines," he says, "becoming more or less just suppliers of raw produce. If the relationship between management and the market becomes too dominant, the real purpose for the cooperative will have been abandoned.

"This creates erosive forces," In 't Veld concludes. "This organizational form runs the risk of becoming a rather loosely-knit, unstable association. In other words, management takes over."

Managing stress

The cooperative members and managers can influence which category of organization fits their business, says Professor in 't Veld. "The cell (category) you occupy is partly determined by the situation you find yourself in. That is a given. But that is also partly determined by strategy," he says.

Organizations that fit more than one category are treading on dangerous ground, he warns. "Some researchers would go so far as to say that organizations that occupy two or more (categories) are doomed." At the same time, he adds, many organizations do occupy more than one category. The issue then becomes how the organization identifies risks and how it handles them.

"An example might be helpful," he says. "Take, for example, the marketing functions of a capacity-oriented organization and compare them to those of a product-oriented organization:

"Let's say, for argument's sake, we're talking about a shoe manufacturer," In 't Veld explains in comparing categories.

In a product-oriented organization, marketing effort is focused on whether the shoes you design and produce can be marketed. This type of business studies the final consumer and is always on the lookout for new trends.

In contrast, the capacity-oriented organization is focused on finding clients who want to place orders for at least 50,000 pairs of shoes that the customer has already designed. The second organization, then, doesn't ask questions about the design and marketability of the product.

"This is a completely different approach," he says. "Obviously, it makes no sense to have the same marketing department do the marketing for both strategies. This fact has to be recognized!"

In 't Veld says he finds it tragic when he watches organizations become engulfed in enormous internal conflicts simply because they haven't recognized the incompatible nature of its marketing strategies. A cooperative, he concludes, should be continually "looking itself in the eye" to determine which category it fits, whether it wishes to occupy that category, and , if necessary, to determine how it will manage the tension arising from being in more than one category at once.

Detection / evaluation

It isn't easy to clearly identify, or pinpoint, the category an organization may be occupying, cautions Professor in 't Veld. He suggests a two-step technique for making an evaluation.

"*First*, take a good look at the nature of your external contacts," he says. "Ask yourself, 'How do they perceive me, how do they approach me, and how do they judge the value I add?'" That should generate a variety of answers that will point clearly to the categories that fit the organization. "You need this sort of feedback to be able to pinpoint your position within the matrix," he adds.

"*Next*, if you fit into more than one category, I suggest that you 'tease' out the elements of stress in the situation and investigate whether this stress can be managed or controlled." **(9)** The organization, or cooperative in this instance, concludes that the inherent stress cannot be managed, it should restructure itself to return to the stable culture offered by a single category, he says. By not taking such corrective action, the organization risks certain destruction from the conflict of strategies.

It often appears that management and members cannot agree on which category of organization their cooperative fits, or occupies. "This can lead to all sorts of problems," In 't Veld says. What's more, the conflict becomes even more complicated when members disagree on the mixture of their cooperative's three core values (risk reduction, economic advantage / meritocracy, and the cooperative culture / fairness of income distribution). **(10)**

Disagreements within the membership can occur over issues that appear minor to the broader scope of the organization, he explains. One example that could be found in many countries is whether the cooperative should support a community quality of life activity, such as sponsoring a local amateur sporting team.

"One member might say: 'I'm in this (cooperative) for reducing risks and for my own advantage; municipal government should finance local sport.' Another member might say, 'We should contribute to the regional community and sponsoring fits in with that.'

"So, opinions on specific, practical issues are definitely influenced by the core value that is most important to you," In 't Veld deduced.

Resolving such issues isn't easy within the collaborative culture of a cooperative, says the expert on organizational structures and public administration. But he is emphatic that a cooperative must try to keep such decision-making internal, even if it reaches outside the organization for occasional guidance from consultants.

"I would never hand over this job to outsiders," he says. "A firm should always maintain control over its own destiny ..."

Inevitably, this raises questions about the ability of members to retain such control when European cooperatives have already become international business entities with international memberships, and North American cooperatives are exploring similar developments. There are different forms of governance found within cooperatives, imbedded in national cultures and in national cooperative business laws.

In 't Veld says he's pessimistic that diverse membership groups may be able to unite around common values when the cooperative becomes an international business. But, he says, there are too few facts and too little experience at this point in history to reach firm conclusions.(11)

Cooperatives: an organizational form for the future

There is growing opinion outside the cooperative world that member-owned businesses will inevitably develop into market-oriented organizations with product goals, i.e. Category Four organizations.

The arguments used to support this opinion refer to members losing touch with events taking place within their cooperatives as the scale of its operations increases, In 't Veld says. It then becomes more difficult for members to keep a check on events, he adds, and management then does as it pleases. A justification comes with the saying, "You need management that can't be pushed around."

This may be happening within some organizations, just as some business professors and other observers predict. But In 't Veld says it shouldn't.

"I think that Category Three is a more plausible option," he says. "If you accept the line of thought expressed above, then you are in fact saying the cooperative is doomed. I don't believe that for a moment!"

Instead, Professor in 't Veld offers a scenario in which the agreement of a cooperative's members to collaborate, and live by rules of fair play, becomes a replacement for governments that are now retreating from enforcing business rules of the game. And, it should be noted, this observation brings a fresh perspective to discussions of transaction cost theory and the advantages of cooperatives raised by others in this book.

"I think the cooperative is an organizational form with a future," he says. "To a large degree our collective values have become too 'state-oriented.' Collective agreements outside the governmental sphere have suffered as a result. However, now that the state is losing or relinquishing power, there is a growing need for collective agreements," he explains.

"These agreements are not bound by territory, either. Nation states are. That's why I think collective agreements have a place in tomorrow's world!"

The cooperative is, in fact, an example of a collective agreement that binds people to collaborating on rules of the game and behavior. It derives its vitality from the values triad of risk reduction, economic advantage and fairness of income distribution, as In't Veld notes throughout his comments. The emphasis given each of these three sets of values may change over time, he adds, but sophisticated relationships will always be based on a particular balance of these three.

"Discard one of the component (or sets of values) and the relationship will erode," he warns. And he sees the chances of this happening as greater for organizations in Category Four.

A warning for the next generation

Society's values change, too, In 't Veld says. "The present generation is experiencing the declining years of the felling of liberation from value-laden relationships, the liberation from all those 'musts' that were imposed on them. The next generation will have never known the restrictions of those 'musts'. For them, all relationships are pallid, devoid of any emotional investment."

The consequences of these changes of values and the period of transition can be great, the professor warns. "I expect an enormous reaction to this. Already, you can observe all sorts of pathological responses: the return of nationalism, racism, sectarianism and regionalism. Another, less pathological reaction can also be seen: 'I want to restore my collective values to their place of honor!'"

In this latter response, he says, society is again orienting its values in a cooperative form.

As a result, In 't Veld concludes, Category Four is not an appropriate "end-point" or stage of development for a cooperative enterprise, especially in light of the macroeconomic driving forces that cause constant change within an organization. At the same time, he says, occupying Category 4 on his matrix doesn't imply that a cooperative is being transformed into a non-cooperative form of business. That is too "evolutionary" a conclusion, he says. By being in Category Four, however, the cooperative should know that dangers lie in depersonalizing members' relationships.

"The result is a weakening of the moderation of self-interest," he says. "Once the relationship between members and their cooperative is no longer value-laden, those members will become hungry and thirsty, all at once. They will want more profit. If you can't deliver, they will look for another who can. That's the end of you (your cooperative), because another can almost always be found."

Chapter Footnotes

1. This is apparently the case worldwide as cooperatives and other business structures compete for the same educated and trained business managers. But it seems especially true in the United States where few modern managers have the missionary-like zeal of early cooperative leaders such as Howard Cowden, M.W. Thatcher and Murray Lincoln, to name just three.

2. In the United States, most sect enterprises are operated by communities bound by religious beliefs. A prime example is the Amish.

3. See chapters on Professors North and Hughes for discussions on transaction costs.

4. This may be the current social condition in most of the world's industrialized nations. However, it is probably safe to say that the concept of cooperative collaboration is swimming against the social currents in the United States of the 1980s and 1990s.

5. "Holiday insurance syndrome" is a Dutch variant of what Americans and Canadians would simply call "an insurance fire," or claims for losses for purposes of collecting the insurance settlement.

6. Such settlements, along with seemingly endless litigation, have become major contributors to "transaction costs" for businesses and insurance customers in the United States.

7. Professor in 't Veld refers to a theory that explains organizations and memberships that is widely used by social scientists, including economists.

8. Usually, a clear definition of these values can be found in mission statements adopted by many American cooperatives. Adhering to them, however, may be more difficult than recognizing them.

9. Professor in 't Veld's use of the word "tease" in this instance is beyond common usage in the United States and western Canada. The editors could not, however, find an appropriate synonym. But "tease" is a wonderfully descriptive term if the reader recalls how school children may take some schoolmate's embarrassing incident or source of stress and grind away at it, from several directions.

10. There are clear examples of such frictions taking shape within North American cooperatives. In some cases, memberships divide along generational lines in which older farmers approaching retirement may want the co-op's assets to remain liquid and not tied up in investments for new projects or business sectors; in other cases a division may occur on the status of the member, whether they are established farmers or beginning farmers. Still another emerging conflict, often triggered by interest groups outside the cooperative, comes over issues of vertical integration. In these cases, the distinction becomes blurred between "top down" ownership of agricultural production and "bottom up" units of production owned by farmers

11. Professor in 't Veld's point is well taken. The editors would note that many early adventures into international operations have been achieved two ways: First, national or regional cooperatives have simply bought the assets of a food or agribusiness company in another country. The local farmers who supply raw products to these foreign investment properties do not become members of the parent cooperative. Second, and perhaps more consistent with cooperative values, a cooperative goes international by creating a joint venture business with a cooperative in another country. The mission of the joint venture can be more narrowly focused and can operate consistent with issues of cultures and governance found within the parent cooperatives.

DR. VERNON W. RUTTAN

Professor Dr. Vernon W. Ruttan is Regents professor at the University of Minnesota in the United States. He and Professor Yujiro Hayami, who is now at Aoyama Gekuia University in Japan, are the principle architects of the Induced Innovation Theory of economic development. It is used by economists to interpret the role and direction of growth, and to guide agricultural research in different countries and cultures around the world.

Professor Ruttan has a B.A. degree from Yale University, Master's and Ph.D. degrees from the University of Chicago, and has taught economics at the University of Minnesota, Purdue University in Indiana, the University of California at Berkeley, and the University of the Philippines. He is a past president of the American Agricultural Economics Association and served on boards for the U.S. Agency for International Development, the Technical Advisory Committee to the Consultative Group on International Agricultural Research, the International Service for National Agricultural Research, and the Board of Global Change for the National Academy of Sciences / National Research Council. He was a staff economist for President Kennedy's Council of Economic Advisers, was president of the Agriculture Development Council that merged with Winrock International, and was agricultural economist for the Rockefeller Foundation at the International Rice Research Institute in the Philippines.

He is author of Agricultural Development: an International Perspective, with Professor Hayami (Johns Hopkins University Press, 1971 and 1985); Agricultural Research Policy, (University of Minnesota Press, 1982); Agriculture, Environment and Health: Sustainable Development in the 21st Century, (University of Minnesota Press, 1994); U.S. Development Assistance Policy: the Politics of Foreign Economic Assistance, (Johns Hopkins University Press, 1996); and more than 100 published studies and chapters for collaborative books.

Professor Ruttan has been elected a Fellow of the American Agricultural Economics Association, the American Academy of Arts and Sciences, the American Association for the Advancement of Science, and to membership in the National Academy of Sciences. His research has received six awards from the American Agricultural Economics Association, the U.S. Department of Agriculture Distinguished Service Award (1986), and the Alexander von Humboldt Award for Outstanding Contribution to Agriculture (1984). He holds honorary degrees from Rutgers University (1978), Christian Albrechts University of Kiel (1986) and Purdue University (1990).

A LOOK AT INDUCED INNOVATION:

The role of resources, culture, technology and institutions in changing markets and changing cooperatives.

By Lee Egerstrom

The letter from the government in the spring of 1943 informed a young Vernon Ruttan he wouldn't return to college classes that fall. Uncle Sam wanted him. He had completed his first year of college and was working that summer on the Ruttan family farm in Michigan. But America was at war; the future economist's education would need to wait while he served in the U.S. Army.

Years later, Professor Ruttan says being pulled away from the family farm for World War II proved informative for his career studying economic development issues. "When the extra hand went off to war, my father decided it was time to buy a tractor. Horses weren't an attractive option when I wasn't there to work them," he says. "That is basic induced innovation."

As Professor Ruttan recalls it, his labor was inexpensive so his father substituted the young man's labor for the investment cost of new technology. "Farmers in Illinois and Iowa bought tractors 20 years earlier. Their land costs were higher than in our area of northern Michigan, and there was a labor shortage in some parts of Iowa and Illinois as young men went to work at industry jobs in Chicago and other cities."

Looking back, the economist remembers farmers in southern Michigan had also bought tractors long before his father and his neighbors. The southern Michigan farms were closer to Detroit, the automobile manufacturing center of the United States, so farmers had to pay competitive labor costs with the auto industry or substitute technology for labor.

In this seemingly simple form, the theory of induced innovation was formed. When labor costs rise, farmers and managers of industry are encouraged to invest in technical innovations; when labor costs are low, such investments aren't induced and innovations may be constrained.

Dutch agriculture has been making similar adjustments to production factors "going back to the days when farmers were using shovels to dig out and build polders by hand. The Dutch, and the Danes for that matter, have some of the severest land constraints on agriculture that you can find in the developed world," he says.

But those aren't the only constraints on agriculture in the Northern European countries, he notes. Adding to the challenge of Dutch and Danish agriculture are Northern Europe's political economy, industrial success and standards of living. These factors make labor costs high compared with competitive agricultural systems in less developed countries, and they lead to family farm income objectives that are set well above income levels tolerated by peasant entrepreneurs in other areas of the world.

Combined, these forces induce technical innovations in Dutch agriculture and institutional innovations by Dutch farmers, he said during an interview at his office at the University of Minnesota's campus in St. Paul, Minnesota.

The same types of constraints and inducements play out in North America, sometimes regionally and sometimes nationally where comparative costs are influenced by world markets

Technical and institutional innovations

Regarding technical innovation, the linkage of Dutch land constraints and labor costs inducing innovation is easy to see, he says, and is consistent with his early research work with Professor Yujiro Hayami when the latter was with Tokyo Metropolitan University in Japan. They compared different paths to agricultural development in Japan and the United States and, later, the Philippines and other countries and regions of the developing world.(1)

Less easy to see and understand for casual observers is induced institutional innovation, he says, although it was responsible for the 1995 National Agriculture Debate among farmers, academics, policy makers and cooperatives in the Netherlands. It was also responsible for a major rewriting of American farm policies late in 1995 and early 1996.

"You have to ask, 'Why are things happening now?' 'Why is there pressure on the cooperatives to merge, restructure, or to move all the way down (or up) to the grocery store with value-added products?'

"If I was over in the university's business school, I would be asking about what is going on inside the cooperative. What is going on inside is a response to what is happening on the outside. It is a response to external inducements."

The economist can identify many of these external inducements. On the technology side, they are the dramatic reductions in the costs of transportation and communications, or information, he says. On the institutional side, the new agricultural accords in the General Agreement on Tariffs and Trade are one. Another is the change in the political economy of nations, and especially the industrialized nations, that is lifting consumer interests relative to producer interests. Enlargement of the European Union plays a part. And for Western European countries, such as the Netherlands, the near-term marketing opportunities that are opening in Eastern Europe and the longer-term threat of trade competition from these same emerging countries are also inducements for change.

At the same time, Professor Ruttan says, there are less apparent reasons for the timeliness of institutional innovations. "Why are the Dutch addressing these issues now when cooperatives in other countries are waiting for something to happen? And why are Northern Europeans so committed to cooperatives when co-ops are typically less developed in other countries?"

The role of culture

The veteran educator asks these questions rhetorically, seizing the moment to educate his interviewer. The answers are found in cultural influences, which he calls cultural endowments, that shape individualized responses even when reasons for technical or institutional innovations are the same for many industries and nations.

In a recently published book, Professors Ruttan and Hayami outlined needed areas of further study on induced innovation that would help everyone experiencing or contemplating change to look inward at their cultural endowments. Among such reasons for more study, they note, their theory works best in explaining the rate and direction of institutional change when it occurs. It doesn't explain why institutional change does not occur or falters in other countries or regions.(2)

In the United States, he says, farmers in northern states respond to changes in the agricultural economy and to trade with different models of cooperatives – often in ways similar to Northern Europe. Farmers in the American South, meanwhile, were slower in developing cooperative businesses and only later and less completely turned to co-ops as instruments of innovation. Regional differences in Europe are equally pronounced, he adds. And some countries of the world, including many that were former colonies of European nations, have been less successful in using cooperatives as institutions for economic development.

Development agencies and economists need to do more work in designing cooperatives in a manner consistent with local cultural endowments, he says.

The Ruttan-Hayami Model of Induced Innovation:

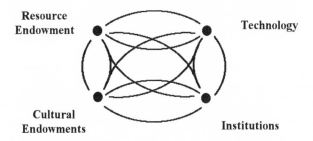

(Graphic by Marisa Egerstrom)

Where work along that line is happening in the United States, it is driven by economic development concerns and by development economists – not by interest in cooperatives and cooperative specialists. An example is current research in the United States where an economist is searching for reasons why former British and Spanish colonies developed along different institutional paths and at different speeds, Professor Ruttan says. This research may be more helpful in North and South America than for researchers and institutions on the European continent. But it is typical of current research that can help firms and cooperative managers understand cultural differences to select induced technical and institutional responses. This is especially so for the large cooperatives – in Europe and the United States – that are becoming multinational businesses with partners, subsidiaries and joint venture operations in other countries.

Though work on induced innovation may be incomplete, the Ruttan-Hayami theory has developed into a model showing interrelationships among the forces that induce change. These forces can be described by four categories that include resource endowments, such as land and labor costs at the Ruttan family farm; cultural endowments, which shape the capacity to respond; technology, such as the availability of a tractor; and institutions. The final category can be as diverse as land tenure relationships, national or European Union farm programs, membership in a cooperative that encourages farmers to produce certain crops or raise certain types of livestock, or environmental regulations that may constrain how farmers farm and what they produce.

At a minimum, a look back at the induced innovation work by Professors Ruttan, Hayami and others around the world should help farmers and their cooperatives reach consensus on their resource endowments, cultural endowments, technology and institutions that will induce or constrain change in their farm and food economy.

This is especially true for those farmers and cooperative managers who realize they have the option of taking action now – and thus stay ahead of global economic changes – or wait until change is forced on them. The risk in the latter option, regardless of type of company ownership, is that forced change from delayed action may limit the company's choices even though the cooperative's farmer-members or the stock company's investors may then more clearly understand the need for change.

Background to studying change

While working as an agricultural economist at Purdue University in 1963, Professor Ruttan listened to a lecture from a visiting British economist, H.J. Habakuk, who was studying reasons why American industrial companies were investing in labor saving technology before their rival firms in Great Britain. American industrial labor costs were higher than comparable wages and salaries then being paid in London, Liverpool and Birmingham. Could it be that American industrialists were buying machines to substitute for labor for the same reason the Ruttan family bought a tractor?

Ruttan pondered that question as he left Purdue University and went to work as staff economist for the International Rice Research Institute in the Philippines. He began reading research papers on technical change written by Professor Hayami in Japan. And he began observing plant scientists from different countries working in the experimental rice fields at the IRRI plots. Both experiences would lead Ruttan to Hayami and the start of a quarter century of collaboration on induced technical innovation.

"When I got to the Philippines, I saw scientists produce different rice yields that didn't make sense to me. The American agronomist's rice yields initially increased, then leveled off. A Japanese plant breeder's yields showed a classic 'S' curve and produced different results. When we reviewed what they did to produce their crops, we saw that both the American and the Japanese brought cultural endowments to the rice project.

"The Japanese responded as farmers would in Japan, where farm labor was less costly at that time. The American responded the way farmers would in the United States, using herbicides to replace labor," he recalls.

The key difference was the way the two visiting scientists responded to weeds in the rice fields. When weeds began growing and threatening the nutrient supply for rice plants, the Japanese sent people into the fields to kill the weeds by pushing the weed plants back into the mud. The American scientist responded by spraying herbicides that killed the weeds while also stunting and killing some of the rice plants.

A bit later, Ruttan began making stops in Tokyo to visit with Hayami. The latter would join Ruttan on the faculty of the University of Minnesota in 1967 through 1969 before he also served a tour of duty as economist for the IRRI in Manila. They began working on induced innovation models and used the history of rice production in East Asia as the subject of their early work (3). Coincidentally, they discovered that neither the IRRI's American nor Japanese scientists responded to weeds the way farmers would in other rice producing countries.

As their work progressed, they extended their analysis beyond technical innovations to exploring institutional innovations as well. The Rockefeller Foundation provided them fellowships to work on their model of induced institutional change, described earlier, at the foundation's Bellagio Center in Italy (4). Professor Hayami has used that work as a foundation to go on and study protectionist Japanese and other

Asian trade policies; Professor Ruttan has applied the model to studying issues of agricultural research policy (5).

That brings up issues that may have set the foundation for the 1995 National Agricultural Debate in the Netherlands, the re-evaluation of national farm policies throughout the industrialized world, and the examination of future business options by Dutch cooperatives. Europe's acceptance of new GATT limitations on agricultural subsidies and trade barriers offers a case in point.

For comparison, Ruttan cites the mood in America by the late 1960s. "It was apparent to everybody (in the United States) that we had to compete and produce for the global market," Ruttan says. Through a referendum of farmers, policies that would have continued supply-management restrictions on farm production were rejected. "Until then, we had agricultural policies that ignored global markets and tried to balance domestic food supplies with demand, as if we were insulated from the world."

A system of target prices and government-operated commodity storage programs was implemented for which farmers could use the stored commodities as collateral for government supplied, short-term loans. This is essentially the U.S. farm program that remained in place for most of the past 30 years, until the 1996 farm program, although elements of supply-management production limitations also survived.

European farmers may not have made a similar decision through elections, but their governments decided for them through reductions in Common Agriculture Policy program benefits, beginning in the mid-1980s, and through agricultural trade concessions internally within Europe and externally in the GATT agreement.

Inherent in the policy changes is a public policy shift away from supporting producers to encouraging consumer-driven markets, Ruttan says. "I haven't explored it, but my intuition is that European governments where forced to ask themselves how much they were willing to pay farmers to keep cows walking around in fields," he says. Placed against the Hayami and Ruttan model, changes in resource endowments and technology that were producing surplus agricultural commodities, and changes in cultural endowments that reflect Europe's overwhelming urban population, were interacting to force change on institutions such as the Common Agriculture Policy (CAP).

Japan and generational change

In Japan, for instance, consumers were willing to pay more than comparable world food prices to support farmers as long as there was extremely rapid industrial growth and their personal incomes kept rising. Moreover, he adds, Japanese farmers "enjoyed a lot of good will. Consumers had a good feeling about farmers because the farmers helped keep them from starving during the war. Those thankful people are in their 70s now, and the next generation doesn't have the same appreciation for farmers.

"It can't be that much different in Europe!"

Generational changes, then, are influences changing both the cultural endowments and institutions that have supported European agriculture, just as surely as they have elsewhere. Policy changes that favor consumers will produce benefits for European farmers as well, but Ruttan concedes that these benefits "are not as obvious in Europe as they were to American farmers in the late 1960s. With Europe opening up, some exports will decline; and some imports will increase. The effects will not be neutral for all farmers and commodities. Some will gain and some will loose."

Many agricultural observers – this writer among them – would argue that broadly based policies such as U.S. farm programs and Europe's CAP could never achieve equitable treatment for all farmers. Balancing competitive interests of butter with olive oil must be an interesting adventure in Brussels. Land constraints, and their related environmental constraints on farming, are more severe in the Netherlands and thus make Dutch resource endowments different from other European countries. CAP policies notwithstanding, Europeans must adjust to differences within the European Union. And some countries, as Professor Ruttan already noted of Denmark and Holland, have already made innovations in response to resource constraints.

"The Dutch have substituted knowledge for resources," he says. While that applies to all of Dutch agriculture, he cites the country's flower industry as a good example. He's watched Dutch farmers ship starter crops of chrysanthemums to Indonesia that would later be finished in Holland and readied for the flower auctions. Modern transportation technology is among the innovations that allow Dutch farmers to change production methods and retain their 70 percent share of the world cut flower market, he says.

Research and development

Research and development programs, and institutions such as Dutch flower auction cooperatives, give Dutch farmers the lead position in the world flower trade. While farmers will need to continue support for their cooperatives' marketing innovations, it will be extremely important for the farmer-members to maintain and support strong research and development programs if they are to survive and prosper in trade-dependent markets.

Continued support for agricultural research may be one of the biggest challenges facing Dutch farmers, Ruttan warns. He's aware that the Netherlands government is considering a retreat from public support for such research and has plans to privatize experiment stations. The British have already gone a long way in this direction, he says. Public support for research during times of relative abundance is declining. And public research expenditures are under attack in governments throughout the world as lawmakers apportion tax dollars. Those pressures apply to multinational institutions as well **(6)**.

Returns on research investment

Agriculture research has produced among the highest returns on investment for taxpayers of all industry sectors, Ruttan insists. In the United States, the majority of fundamental, or basic, research is publicly supported and conducted at research universities or U.S. Department of Agriculture Experiment Stations that are often closely associated with state (provincial) research universities.

"I've often mentioned to deans of agriculture that they should be ashamed of their high rates of return on agricultural research. The high returns indicate an underinvestment in research!

"If the rate of return on research at 3M Company (also based at St. Paul, Minnesota) was as high as 50 percent, as it sometimes is with agriculture, the president would be fired! It would indicate that the president was not growing the company fast enough. You deans who run the colleges of agriculture have to show investors – the taxpayers – how research is helping you 'grow the company'."

Despite the track record of research around the world, expenditures for private sector food-related research lag behind research budgets for other industries, he says. "Less than one percent of food industry sales is spent on research and development. From 8 to 12 percent of sales is used on research in the chemicals and pharmaceuticals industries.

"The average expenditures on research for all industries in the United States are about two percent most years," Ruttan says. "That isn't great."

That brings Professor Ruttan back to current Dutch plans. "If I was a Dutch farmer, I would worry about the effects of privatizing national research institutions, or experiment stations, unless good plans have been made to find other methods to support fundamental and applied agricultural research."

If the Dutch follow the paths already taken in other countries, industry will support applied research in areas that can produce proprietary products. Fundamental research and applied research that cannot be embodied in a proprietary product will have fewer supporters and friends, he warns, even though fundamental research may provide greater long-term returns on research investments. Cooperatives may see the long-term benefits in supporting this research, Ruttan adds. But private companies and multinational stock companies aren't as likely. "The question for them is whether it makes any difference where they source (buy) their raw products."

For Ruttan, an important challenge facing farmers and their cooperative businesses will be in helping maintain national or regional cultures that support institutional assistance to research. Again citing a Dutch example, the National Agricultural Debate project was a fundamental research experiment on the future shape and direction of Dutch agriculture. Implied in this national discussion was an attempt to plan and bring order to what Ruttan and Hayami call induced innovation. Whatever becomes of Dutch agriculture and its many sectors, it will result from conflicts and interrelationships between external and internal influences of resources, culture, technology and institutions.

Given all the international influences converging on agriculture worldwide and the shifting of institutional support for agriculture, Ruttan says he understands why the Dutch initiated a national dialogue on the future of agricultural technology, institutions and policies.

"What I can't explain is why other countries are so far behind," he says.

Chapter Footnotes

1. Hayami, Yujiro and Ruttan, Vernon W. <u>Agriculture Development: An International Perspective</u>. (Baltimore: Johns Hopkins University Press, 1971 and 1985.)

2. Ruttan, Vernon W. and Hayami, Yujiro. "Induced Innovation Theory and Agricultural Development. A Personal Account." Published in: Koppel, Bruce M. (Editor). <u>Induced Innovation Theory and International Agricultural Development: A Reassessment</u>. (Baltimore: Johns Hopkins University Press, 1995).

3. Ruttan, Vernon W. and Hayami, Yujiro. "Korean Rice, Taiwan Rice, and Japanese Agricultural Stagnation: An Economic Consequence of Colonialism." *Quarterly Journal of Economics*. (November, 1970.)

4. Recalled during an interview. For another account, see: Koppel. <u>Induced Innovation Theory and International Agriculture Development: A Reassessment</u>.

5. Ibid.

6. See: Ruttan, Vernon W. <u>Agricultural Research Policy</u>. (University of Minnesota Press, 1982.)

PART THREE: PERSPECTIVES ON CHANGE AND GLOBAL MARKET POWER

CHARTING COURSES FOR COOPERATIVES IN TIMES OF CHANGE

PROFESSOR DR. JESPER STRANDSKOV

A VIEW FROM DENMARK

Professor Dr. Jesper Strandskov (born 1954) lectures on international business at Aarhus School of Business in Denmark. Upon completing his studies in economics at the University of Copenhagen in 1980, he became an assistant to Denmark's European Union agriculture commissioner, Finn Olav Gundelach, in Brussels. In 1982, Professor Strandskov began lecturing in business economics at Copenhagen School of Business, specializing in the internationalization of business. All the while he was lecturing, his interest in the food sector grew. In particular, the sector's macro-economic and agricultural policy aspects attracted his attention.

Professor Strandskov has twice left academia to work as a management consultant for PA International where he specialized in foodstuffs industries. For the past six years he has been actively involved in the management of abattoirs (animal slaughter and processing plants) and meat processing. He sits as an expert on a number of official committees that are closely involved with decision making and industry studies. Among the latter are studies of structural and strategic problems concerning the concentration, marketing, innovation and internationalization of cooperative agribusinesses in Denmark.

Among his extensive list of published works are studies on internationalization of business, the European Union's Common Agricultural Policy (CAP), and the Danish dairy industry, for which he has received several research awards.

"FIRST MERGE NATIONALLY (REGIONALLY), THEN PENETRATE THE ENTIRE PRODUCTION-MARKETING CHAIN..."
By Dr. Gert van Dijk with Dr. Jan Werts

It is a long road leading from the birth of a piglet to the moment when a tasty slice of bacon or sausage is placed on our plates. From experience we know that value is added at each stage along the way, and that each stage yields proportionately more profit. At the first stage the farmer, as supplier of the raw product, receives only modest returns on investment and labor. The abattoir (1) can also expect only a moderate return for its input. Higher up the food chain, however, in the production and marketing of a variety of fine-tasting processed meats of guaranteed high quality, real profits are usually the greatest.(2)

This is the case for the entire marketing chain, right up to the sale of the product. The farther up the chain, the greater the relative profit. This is not only so for pork, but for all farm produce – much of which is marketed through agricultural cooperatives in Western industrialized countries.(3)

This then raises questions how a regional or national cooperative can move closer to the consumer and reach further up the chain to where more profits can be found. This is especially so for cooperatives that have concentrated on the slaughter of pigs or making of cheese and butter from milk, which adds little value to the farmers' product. How can these cooperatives establish a place for themselves in international markets? And how can members of the cooperative be convinced they need to invest in such ventures?

Given the importance of these questions to farmers and their agribusiness cooperatives throughout the world, they were made the subject of an interview with Dr. Jesper Strandskov, professor of international business at the Aarhus School of Business in Denmark.

The situation in Denmark

"Towards the end of the last century, farmers in Denmark established local dairy cooperatives and cooperative abattoirs. Over the past two decades, however, there has been an overwhelming trend towards concentration, so that today there are only five abattoirs – actually pork cooperatives – and a few dairy factories," says Strandskov in painting a broad-brush picture of Danish agriculture.

"The two biggest dairy cooperatives are, in order of size, MD Foods and Klovermaelk. Taking the two together, one could speak of a monopoly. Nevertheless, after much hemming and hawing by the Danish government and the European Union, they have been given permission – despite the resulting reduction of competition – to closely coordinate their activities on the national market for milk ... and related (dairy) products," he adds. "I would not be at all surprised if these two don't merge at some time in the future, giving them control of more than 90 percent of the Danish market. What is left will be served by a handful of specialized, privately-owned companies."

Aside from questions about concentration, however, this consolidation and business expansion have occurred despite a reluctance by Danish farmers to invest in their cooperative businesses, says Strandskov. "Farmers are not inclined to invest heavily in their own cooperatives. They would rather invest in their own farm businesses, which already depend on outside capital (loans), for which they must bear the burden of high interest payments," he says. "For this reason, cooperatives in Denmark have sometimes been forced to look to pension funds for the capital they require."

MD Foods, for example, established MD Foods International in this way to expand its marketing operations, he says. This move gave MD Foods access to British agribusiness that includes five large dairy factories that supply milk to consumers. "To date, the returns have been poor," Strandskov observes.

Meanwhile, he said, cooperatives in the slaughtering industry formed Tulip International. "As in the dairy industry, 40 to 50 percent of the capital for this venture came from investments by pension funds," Strandskov explains. Both MD Foods International and Tulip International have ventured into product development and international marketing for their cooperative members. Both were organized as investor-owned firms. The larger cooperatives hold the majority of the shares; a minority is in the hands of the pension funds.(4)

Strandskov notes that dairy farmers have shown more willingness to invest in their dairy cooperatives than pig farmers to invest in their abattoirs in recent decades. "That's why MD Foods has been able to internationalize over the past quarter century; they are ahead of the slaughtering cooperatives," he said.

Confusing competition, concentration and countervailing power

The entire pork industry in Denmark is controlled by five abattoirs, including names of cooperative companies that may be well known to consumers in other European countries and in North America, Strandskov says. Danish Crown is particularly strong in the east and south of Denmark. Vestjyske is most active in western Jutland. Combined, they account for more than two-thirds of the 21 million pigs slaughtered annually in Denmark. Live exports of pigs to abattoirs elsewhere, as is done on a large scale in the Netherlands, is not common in Denmark, he adds. He identified other abattoirs operating in Denmark include Stiff, Hoklberg and the smaller TICAN.

"The problem now," Strandskov continues, " is that these five cooperatives compete fiercely amongst themselves when buying pigs for slaughter. That reduces profits, preventing them from creating the capital reserves they need to internationalize their operations or to develop and market more products."

But that is only one level of the problems facing Danish cooperatives, as Strandskov sees it. In his penetrating analysis of the Danish pork situation, he cites problems facing cooperative businesses in other successful agricultural nations as well.

"Just as in the Netherlands, nearly three-quarters of production is exported," he says. "Five slaughtering cooperatives that are regularly getting in each other's way is, in my opinion, far too many. Not so long ago an attempt was made to merge them into one large abattoir. Unfortunately, the negotiations foundered," he says.

"Perhaps the personal interests of certain board members – many pig farmers sit on their boards – and managers were better served by allowing the situation to continue."

Danish cooperatives "at a crossroads"

Danish farmers are regarded in North America, at least, as the world's most successful pork producers and exporters. Professor Strandskov, nevertheless, speaks of need for change to maintain this leadership position. That the above changes haven't happened, he suspects, is because current conditions in Danish pork markets aren't "bad enough" to cause a will to change.

Regardless, he says, the marketing of Denmark's important pork and dairy commodities "is at a crossroads. I expect that within a period of 10 years the European foodstuffs market will be dominated by (from) seven to 10 retail-marketing chains. It is vital to Danish agribusiness to be able to negotiate with these giants on an equal footing," he says.

To accomplish this, Strandskov says, farmers' cooperatives must improve their market position and develop a range of gourmet meat and dairy products. Too much emphasis is given to slaughtering and basic milk and dairy processing, he says; and too little attention is given to developing and launching gourmet products with higher value-added content.

"To make matters worse, the European Union milk quotas are forcing cuts in milk production; (and) the pig farmer (cannot) expand. In short, capacity is being reduced.," he says.

"In response to these threats, a committee has been formed to study the Danish agricultural cooperative sector in the hope of providing a clear view of future developments and so point to a way out of the present impasse," Strandskov says. The committee is designing four models of development policy from which, eventually, choices may be made within the cooperative sector. "Our aim is to market milk and pork in such a way as to maximize profit for the declining number of farmers," he explains, referring to the 40,000 dairy farmers and 25,000 pig producers that remained in 1995. "In fact, we are really talking about 4,000 of Denmark's largest and most modern farm businesses, which dominate Danish pig and dairy farming," he adds.

Retail and international brands

Currently, says Professor Strandskov, food marketing in Europe is being divided into four types of brands that reflect the companies that own them. They are:

+ Multinational brands, such as the product lines from Unilever and Nestle;
+ Large, national well-known brands; (5)
+ Large, export-oriented brands, among them products from Danish and Dutch cooperatives; and
+ Smaller, national or local gourmet brands.(6)

The multinational brands are widely available in geographical terms. They have a high market profile and direct access to consumers through retail outlets, Strandskov says. The large national brands also have a strong market position but they are less widely available. The brands belonging to the third group have a wide geographic distribution but they do not as yet enjoy a high market profile, he adds. And the smaller gourmet brands are neither widely distributed nor well positioned in the market. (7)

"The issue now, due to slow growth in European consumption, is who is going to capture whose share of the market? Retail chains are consolidating more and more, and that trend will continue because their operating margins are slight, particularly in Germany and France,"

Strandskov says. "To strengthen their market position these chains develop their own brands. The consumer may compare and choose: chain brands are often 20 to 30 percent cheaper than the (name brands) and that appears to make a difference."

Strandskov estimates that from 25 to 30 percent of the turnover in the foodstuffs market is generated by retail-chain brands in some European countries, in particular the United Kingdom; and to a lesser extent in Germany and France. This trend is being caused by three influences converging on the foodstuffs market, he adds: new products, cheaper products and more products.

Who pays the bill?

"Who has had to foot the bill for this abundance?" Strandskov asks rhetorically. "Thanks to fierce competition, (it's) not the consumer. The distributor? No, certainly not. No, it is more likely to be the producer. The cooperative, in fact, and ultimately the farmer whose margins have already been steadily shrinking."

A close look at the dairy and meat sectors in Northern Europe, and similar sectors of foodstuffs, shows three modes of marketing, he says. On one end of the spectrum are the specialized areas of the meat sector within the EU, numbering about 2,000 manufacturers, he says. Most are family-owned firms that concentrate on one specific product, such as ham. At the other end of the spectrum are the multinationals. "They buy their raw products in bulk, at the lowest price available. In between you find the cooperatives. I would be not at all surprised if, in the future, these multinationals develop European-wide brands and through integrated marketing try to increase their share of the market," he explains. This is what the multinationals have already done within the U.S. market stretching from the Atlantic to Pacific oceans.

"Advertising on international television channels, in particular, will play a great role in achieving this," he predicts. "The multinationals are at a great advantage: rapid access to retail outlets, expert knowledge of the markets, the means to inundate European consumers with brand advertising, and the ability to profit from considerable economies of scale."

This will bring the multinationals in direct competition with national brands, just as it did earlier in the United States. In the Netherlands, for example, Strandskov says the companies in the path of the multinationals are the two to three large dairy cooperatives that control the Dutch market. (7) The national brands, including many that are products of cooperatives, thus face the prospect of fierce competition on two fronts, he adds: "The retail chain brands on one side; and on the other, the multinationals."

The weapon of competitive pricing

Consumers will notice when the battle is joined over winning market shares for dairy and meat products, Strandskov says. "The battle will be fought with the six weapons commonly found in this sort of conflict: marketing mix, price, product, distribution, promotion, product portfolio, and strategic alliances.

"Seen from the level of the farm gate and the first stage of processing, we often say – cynically – that the weapons will be price, price, price ... and again ... price. The majority of consumers can distinguish little difference in the quality of the meat and dairy products being offered. The same holds true for the quality of pork coming from different countries," he says. As an example, he notes, Denmark's pork products are standardized, competitively priced, and have been noted in the past for their quality. The difference in quality is not so marked anymore, he adds, citing the harmonization of veterinary practices promoted in the European Union and within the General Agreement on Tariffs and Trade regulations. (8)

"Nevertheless, in terms of structural development within the dairy and meat sectors, Denmark is still a leader. From this advantageous position, the task at hand is to develop products that will meet the demands of tomorrow's consumers," continues the business professor. Because neither consumers nor the distribution chains are inclined to bear the cost of such development, the burden is passed by default down the chain to the lowest stage of the production process, he says. This is especially so at the level of the cooperative abattoir. "There is no one else left," he said of the process of handing down such development costs.

"Unfortunately, the organization and efficiency at this stage are already optimal so there is no margin to be created from which to meet these increases in cost," he observes. "Who, then, will carry the burden for more market development? Who, then, can be found to invest in new products, new markets and new concerns (business ventures)? (9)

Adding to the burden of the smaller and national cooperatives is the reduction in trade barriers under the GATT and reform of the European

Union's Common Agriculture Policy, Strandskov adds. This, he predicts, will put more pressure on prices farmers receive from their milk and meat at the same time they should be investing in more product development work.

"My conclusion: the large dairy and meat cooperatives will have to come up with a new strategy. Gradually, they will have to extend their activities beyond slaughtering and processing, to develop expensive product brands in their sectors," he says. "This will require enormous investments, not only for new products but also to acquire foreign companies, or even found new ones..."

Up until now, Strandskov says, Danish farmers' activities have been limited to expansion into the United Kingdom. They may look to starting new ventures in Eastern Europe, for example, where environmental regulations and labor costs are not prohibitive for entering the market. In brief, he says, "cooperatives can no longer restrict their operations solely to the slaughter of pigs and the processing of milk. However, this will require existing cooperatives to merge, forming one, at the most two, national cooperatives."

Farm debt in Denmark

Cooperative boards in Denmark, which have the final say in investment issues, are convinced that these sorts of changes are necessary, Strandskov says. "The problem is that there is a shortage of funds to implement them. Danish farmers are often carrying large debts. To them, revenue left in the cooperative is not a long-term investment, but rather an extra cost they well could do without," he says.

Developing markets outside Denmark will take time, he adds, estimating at least five years. Farmer-members want their money back quickly, as well as a high return on investment. "This can be seen every autumn when the dairy manufacturers and abattoirs make their supplementary payments," he says. "Woe betide the cooperative that falls behind its competitors; they won't win the popularity stakes!"

Competition among the cooperatives to pay the highest prices for milk or pigs robs the cooperatives of the possibility of accumulating capital reserves needed for product development and market expansion, he says. And it isn't just a Danish problem, he notes. The scene is played out every week in the meat sector in the Netherlands. But the rivalry between cooperatives over which will pay the highest purchase price becomes especially frantic in Denmark at the time for making the annual supplementary payments, he says. "For the rest of the year, all (Danish) cooperatives pay farmers the same prices."

Farm debt problems may be causing Danish farmers to play their cooperatives off against each other for short-term gains from the sale of milk or pigs.(10) This practice, he says, has the unfortunate side-effect of impeding their cooperatives' efforts to develop new products and internationalize.

"If the abattoirs and dairy factories do manage to consolidate, which I don't doubt will happen, the rivalry among cooperatives for the farmers' favor will disappear," he says. Perhaps Danish pig farmers will opt to sell their pigs in Germany, he adds, although they would need to leave their cooperatives to do so given compulsory supply arrangements similar to what farmers in other countries call a "closed cooperative."

"Denmark has one slight advantage over the Netherlands in that there is no overcapacity in Danish abattoirs," he says. "In the dairy sector, the positions are reversed: there is more overcapacity in Denmark than in the Netherlands. Traditionally, the Danish dairy industry has always produced for the global market. Now that the EU export subsidies are gradually being reduced, the Danes will – as the Dutch have always done – have to focus more on EU markets to capture greater (market) share.

"The real question is, however, who is going to invest in this venture?" Strandskov asks. The pressure to change – to do something different – will increase and come at the farmers' cooperatives from the retail industry. "If farmers are not able to invest in their cooperatives, in the long run they will have to accept a lower price for their produce," he warns. "If they do invest, it will mean a higher yield (income return) in their firm in the long run."

Complete vertical integration

Professor Strandskov does see a way out of this dilemma for Danish farmers and producers in other developed countries. "It all boils down to complete vertical integration, from the breeding and fattening of pigs, on through to slaughter and processing of meat, and on to the marketing of entire ranges of products," he says. "Dairy cooperatives, too, must gain control of the entire production and marketing chain."

The Danes have an edge on other European producers in that they have already achieved vertical production and marketing for the Japanese market, he says. The level of farmer-member involvement in this market development has been high. "Moreover, it is an advantage that Danish standard pig quality, which until now has been primarily destined for the British and Japanese markets, is lighter than its German and Dutch counterparts. This pig easily meets the demands made by consumers on the (European) Continent, into which we are gradually expanding our influence," he adds.

To achieve the vertical integration needed, Denmark will need to create the largest pork cooperative in Europe, forecasts Strandskov. It will need annual turnover, or sales revenues of about DKR 35 billion (NLG 42 billion or U.S. $28 billion). Such a cooperative would not need to curry favor with farmers in a bidding price war for pigs, so additional capital resources would be freed up for development of international markets. "I think this event is not too far off," he says. But to position their cooperative for the international market, he adds, pig farmers would need to forego their supplementary payments for several years. "Unfortunately, I do not see them accepting that," he concludes.

Farmers can't afford to invest properly in their abattoirs and meat processing factories, or they don't want to take the risk, Strandskov says. "Capital costs are high in Denmark. In the '80s, many young, progressive farmers took out large loans to modernize and expand their farming operations. At that time interest rates were 20 percent, so these farmers have had to reduce their debt as much as possible," he explains. "They don't have the means at their disposal to invest in their cooperatives. Older farmers, who could often do without their supplementary payments, don't dare take the risk of investing. They are afraid that the returns on product development and internationalization will fall short of expectations," he adds.

Four models for Danish development

Just as Professor Strandskov sees a need for cooperatives to change to keep abreast of changes in the food marketing sector, he sees four logical models for cooperatives to follow in achieving their goals. (His explanations of the four are contained here, but they've been given a description, or name, by the editors to clarify the differences for the reader.)

THE INDEPENDENT, FARMER-OWNED COMPANY –

This model may be the most attractive to farmers at the current time, Strandskov says. One or two large cooperatives will continue to exist in the future as independent firms, possessing their own factories. They will develop and market new consumer products from their members' milk and pork. And institutional investors – pension funds in Denmark – will need to be assured that competition between cooperatives will cease if they are to serve as outside investors.

"Concentration is therefore a prerequisite," he says. "The remaining national cooperatives for milk and pork could establish investor-owned firms for their factories. Nevertheless, Danish farmers will want to retain control of their cooperatives, and probably control of the entire production chain. Thus it is likely that the national dairy and pork cooperatives will demand guarantees that will prevent multinationals, such as Unilever or Nestle, from participating in their company..

"That is something Danish farmers make no bones about. Pension funds and the like are welcome; competitors keep out!" he says.

This creates a dilemma in that the same pig farmers who do not want to bear the risks that come with founding such companies are telling other players in the sector to stay out even though they may be willing to shoulder the risk. Strandskov says it isn't reasonable to expect the pension funds or other passive investors to take the financial risks. So a complete dilemma exists.

But it is at this point that Professor Strandskov pulls a magician's rabbit from his hat.

"In Denmark, the pension funds that have invested in agribusiness often have a large proportion of employee organizations, such as trade unions, represented in their management," he says. This includes the abattoirs. "It is in the interests of these unions that cooperatives modernize, even though the foodstuffs branch is, in terms of yield (returns), certainly no gold mine," he says.(11)

"I've done a few rough calculations on the costs of capturing a greater market share in one of the large EU countries," he explains. He estimate that if one of Denmark's large cooperatives wanted to buy a company already operating in one of these markets, and thus acquire the desired market share, it will cost the cooperative about DKR 4 to 5 billion (NLG 1.5 billion or U.S. $1 billion). For the cooperatives to be able to carry this financial burden, he says, the farmers would need to be prepared to leave about 10 percent of their supplementary payments in their cooperatives during the acquisition period.

That becomes a contentious issue, as Strandskov has already mentioned. But the advantage of this first model is that farmers do maintain control of the production chain. And that, says the Danish business professor, would be reason enough for pig farmers to choose that model – especially if they could be guaranteed returns.

Since the latter guarantees are "out of the question," he says, the dearth of risk-bearing capital has given rise to a second model.

THE INVESTMENT STOCK COMPANY –

This model assumes that Danish cooperatives must internationalize and capture new markets to survive, he says. Abattoirs and milk processors remain in this model under the control of cooperatives, but pig farmers, for example, will relinquish control of processing further along the production chain as the product moves closer to the consumer. Shareholders representing a combination of cooperatives, without majority control, and parties from outside the agricultural sector, such as pension funds, would have minority interests. Essentially, shareholders would hold the reins, not pig farmers in this example. Concurrently, the necessary process of internationalization will be put into motion, he says.

Cooperatives will still have a significant role to play in this model, Strandskov says, although it is no longer the leading one. Perhaps even more than would ever be the case in the first model, Danish farmers would have to ensure that their milk and pork continue to be inexpensive and of high quality. "In the second model, Danish agribusiness is free to import its raw products from anywhere it pleases, even Germany, the Netherlands or United States."

THE STRATEGIC PARTNER COOPERATIVE –

A third model takes agribusiness production and manufacturing a step farther, Strandskov says. In this model, cooperatives would invest primarily in those branches of production that have been their traditional strength, especially the cheap, dependable and high-quality supply of raw produce. Production and marketing farther up the food chain would be in the hands and ownership of other food company players and their owners, he said.(12)

A COMBINATION MODEL –

A fourth model would be a combination of the above, especially of the first two models, says Professor Strandskov. And are there other choices? Yes, he answers, although they become variants of the above.

Danish cooperatives could forge strategic alliances with foreign companies that are in some way similar to them, he notes, just as the Danish ESS-Food cooperative did with the Dutch cooperative Encebe. "Together they were to have processed and cut meat," he explains. "Unfortunately, the initiative foundered due to a sharp drop in the supply of pigs from the Netherlands, and it became more attractive to export pigs live to German markets. This exacerbated the overcapacity already existing in Dutch abattoirs," he says.

"By the way, many Danish pig farmers could not understand how we (Danes) could join forces with the Dutch – one of our strongest competitors. A more or less similar variant would be an alliance with the Swedes, a subject of speculation since Sweden joined the EU. Our MD Foods could combine forces with Arla, the largest dairy cooperative in Sweden, to distribute and market each other's produce."

Cooperatives throughout the European Union have the possibility of forming such strategic alliances among themselves to increase their market influence, he notes. A Dutch cooperative, for instance, that has well-developed marketing channels in Germany or France could form an alliance with a Danish cooperative and, in doing so, improve its penetration of the UK, Danish and Japanese markets. "In this way, each partner could help the other compensate for its weak spot – vulnerable and expensive to maintain marketing and distribution channels – at no visible cost," he explains. "These are the sorts of opportunities that we must create to avoid falling prey to the multinationals."

Cooperatives: their strengths and weaknesses

This leaves behind questions about the comparative strengths and weaknesses of cooperatives as they venture forth into the market place to battle for market share.

"There are plenty of examples of how influential shareholders can destroy companies by stripping them of their profitable components and closing down the rest," Professor Strandskov says. "Take the case of the French firm Olida. It had built up a strong position in the processing of ham, yet it changed hands several times in quick succession. This stands in stark contrast with the trust and commitment typical of members of Danish cooperatives. Their stability and loyalty are a positive force for the entire Danish economy," he adds.

Part of this comes from a healthy cooperative spirit, he explains. Should a cooperative run into serious problems, others would come running to its aid – "if only to prevent it from falling into commercial hands.

"It is this healthy cooperative spirit, together with high levels of member involvement, that leads me to be optimistic about the future of cooperatives," he concludes. "These are two elements that contribute to the strength of Danish agribusiness."

But there are disadvantages, as well, that must be managed, he adds.

Management would benefit from better and more training, he cites as an example. "Management still has too many people whose experience is limited to one firm; people who have slowly climbed the rungs of the internal management ladder.

"Another disadvantage is that too many board members come from the agricultural sector and that they dominate the discussions concerning strategy," Strandskov added. "Fortunately, this is changing as more and more farmers have been educated in universities and polytechnics (institutes). Nevertheless, it makes good sense to include people from other walks of life on supervisory boards," he said, echoing comments from business professors and economists from throughout Europe.

Chapter Footnotes

1. The term "abattoir" is used throughout this chapter, just as it is widely used across the language groups of Europe. For Americans unfamiliar with the French term, it is a slaughter plant, or factory; and it can mean anything from a basic animal kill station to a partial or complete meat processing plant.

2. This can vary from year to year, depending on different livestock cycles. But American livestock farmers were aware of strong processing margins for pork and beef in 1994 through 1996 for publicly traded companies such as Hormel Foods and ConAgra while live animal prices fell below the cost of production on many American farms. The same undoubtedly applied to Farmland Industries' farmers and ranchers and their meat processing operations.

3. Strandskov's description accurately reflects marketing conditions in Europe. American dairy cooperatives do not have similar market

power; and American livestock producers are only beginning to form cooperatives that may achieve future market clout.

4. Professor Strandskov will deal with the role of pension funds later in this chapter. It should be noted that a similar arrangement with pension funds would be illegal in all but the rarest occasions under American fiduciary laws.

5. Americans and Canadians might reflect on the consolidation of their strong regional brands into national and multinational branded food companies in recent years, although little of this activity in brand consolidation has involved cooperatives. The Strandskov models would help Europe's cooperatives position themselves to compete against the multinational food companies' brands in global and continental food markets.

6. For an American example, the successful Land O'Lakes cooperative would most likely fall into this latter category despite its successes in marketing branded dairy products nationally.

7. The suspense of a pending battle for the hearts and taste buds between multinationals and national cooperatives is over in the Netherlands. As tourists in Holland soon discover, the Campina Melkunie cooperative and Dutch-British food conglomerate Unilever are waging battle with frozen dairy desserts from supermarkets, ice cream parlors, petrol stations and sidewalk vendors throughout the nation.

8. The ISO 9000-series of international quality systems certification is adding momentum to harmonization, although its use in the food sector appears to lag behind other manufacturing sectors.

9. An opposite situation exists for American and Canadian farmers. The big food companies do develop new products and aggressively seek new markets. Thus, this burden doesn't fall to the farmer. But North American farmers must also bear this burden if they want to capture a part of the value-added food market.

10. This situation doesn't track with animal marketings in North America. But farmers, who are starting new cooperatives to move closer to the consumer, should ask themselves if their new venture will indeed add value over existing cooperative entities. This is raised, rhetorically, because some Saskatchewan farmers are known to be considering starting a rival grain storage and handling cooperative in the backyard of Saskatchewan Wheat Pool operations, and some farmers in North Dakota and Minnesota are considering a new entity that may duplicate some of the same marketing services provided by Harvest States Cooperatives.

11. As described by Strandskov, the passive investment by pension funds would not be legal in the United States. However, there are community development funds and rural electric utility companies with investment programs that fit this mode, for the same common interests.

12. What Strandskov proposes here fits with the growth of farming supply contracts in the United States. Food companies and meat packers want an assured supply at precise times for processing raw produce such as vegetables and meat animals. Thus, they offer production contracts to growers or animal feeders that assure a future price and acceptance of the farmers' harvest. If current plans for cooperative meat packing companies develop in the Northern Plains, a similar arrangement with non-member producers is also likely.

PROFESSOR JERKER NILSSON

A VIEW FROM SWEDEN

Professor Jerker Nilsson, 50, has been a professor of Cooperative Business Administration at the Swedish Agricultural University at Uppsala since 1989. Over the past 20 years, he has been a prolific writer about management, marketing and the phenomena of cooperatives in Scandinavia.

Born at Malmo, he graduated at the University of Lund in southern Sweden in 1967, becoming an instructor, and he received his graduate degree in 1980 after studying the buying practices of Swedish supermarket chains. Professor Nilsson taught for five years at the Aarhus University School of Business in Denmark, and for seven years at the Copenhagen School of Economics and Business Administration before returning to Sweden to teach Cooperative Business Administration at Uppsala.

Professor Nilsson is a member of the official commission studying the effectiveness of the Swedish cooperative legal code. And he continues to do research on both agricultural and consumer cooperatives. Recently published works include analysis of non-member partners in cooperative organizations, and his book, **Konsum Osterreich: Der Weg in den Untergang**, examines the failure of a poorly managed cooperative.

In addition, he has published a study on new trends in cooperation in **Co-operatives Today**; and elsewhere, he has published articles on competition and cooperation within cooperatives, the concept of a communications plan for a cooperative, and the organization of research within the cooperative structure.

THE COOPERATIVE'S MOST PRECIOUS ASSET: MEMBER INVOLVEMENT

By Dr. Gert van Dijk and Dr. Jan Werts

Cooperative institutions are coming under pressure on several fronts. They are meeting international competition in finding profitable markets for their members' wares. At the same time, they are facing challenges internally from members who see their companies undergoing change, and they may not understand or appreciate the changes; and within their national environments where the public may have lost sight of the historic, or traditional reasons for creating cooperative businesses.

Such may be the case in Sweden, a country with a long history of cooperative involvement in agricultural processing and marketing. And if it can happen in Sweden, it should be a warning to farmers everywhere; the same may be coming to your country and your cooperative organizations.

"At the moment, there is an anti-cooperative mood in Sweden," says Professor Dr. Jerker Nilsson, economics professor at the Department of Economics, Swedish University of Agricultural Sciences in Uppsala.

The Swedish Riksdag (Parliament) launched a national competition policy in 1993 that even puts a ban on the traditional cooperative principle of delivery obligations, he says. And a group of academic, political and business leaders with a bias against cooperatives meets regularly in Stockholm. "These members reproach the cooperatives as being inefficient and distorting the free flow of capital in our market economy because the shares are not freely marketable." Moreover, he says, this group may have influenced the legislation that is now causing the review of competition and competitiveness in Sweden.(1)

Professor Nilsson is one of the most respected observers of cooperative structures, policies and activities worldwide. He comes to the subject from historical reasons: cooperatives in Sweden have a long history. Market shares enjoyed by Swedish cooperatives range from 100 percent, for dairy; to 74 – 79 percent in meats, depending on the product category; to 70 – 79 percent for cereal grains; and 50 percent for forestry.

He, himself, is a member of two governmental commissions evaluating the legislation on competition and on cooperatives, and he is engaged in the cooperative struggle with anti-cooperative forces.

Despite criticism from the cooperative sector, Professor Nilsson does not expect amendments to the legislation on competition, he says. "This means that cooperatives have to apply for permission from the Competition Board if they, for example, want to sign production contracts with their members," he explains. But the chances for getting Swedish law on cooperatives modernized, nevertheless, are brighter.(2)

Among other examples of the anti-cooperative mood in Sweden, he says, include the tax treatment of subordinated debt, or the selling of B-shares, in cooperatives. Interest paid on these shares is not tax deductible, he says; thus, they become virtually useless for capital formation despite great expectations when they were introduced in cooperative law in 1987. And, if a cooperative doesn't have open membership and doesn't apply the principle of one member, one vote, patronage refunds (nabetaling) are not tax deductible.(3) A few years back, Nilsson added, a member of the Swedish Parliament went so far as to propose a change in law allowing 15 percent of a cooperative's membership to transform the company into a public limited, or stock company. The parliamentarian didn't succeed; but, says Nilsson, "That beats everything!"

The arguments of the cooperative critics

The criticism of cooperative business in Sweden is based, among other issues, on the so-called "*agency theory*," Professor Nilsson says. This theory claims there are a number of problems inherent in the form, or structure, of the cooperative organization. Nilsson says they include:

+ The *common property problem*: New members get immediate access to all the assets of the cooperative, and exiting members do not get any share of the value of the cooperative, which means non-optimal decision-making in the cooperative among its members.(4)

+ The *portfolio choice problem*: As all the members have different preferences as to risk, it is impossible for the managers to make investments in the interest of the entire membership.

+ The *horizon problem*: As young and old members have different planning horizons, the cooperative will not make the best investments.

+ The *decision-maker problem*: The managers cannot reasonably know the opinions of a large and diverse membership.

+ The *control problem*: The members are not able to control the managers as the latter have superior information and are more motivated to take action.

The *agency theory* argument is problematic, Nilsson says, in that the theoretical presumptions are not in agreement with cooperative business principles. But it does have some relevance, he adds, and perhaps more so for consumer cooperatives than agricultural cooperatives. "But it cannot be claimed to have general validity for cooperatives!"

Regarding the *common property problem*, critics argue that the cooperative's shares should be tradable at market prices, he explains. If this were done, he cautions, the membership and the volumes would probably be fixed.(5) Such an organization would not be optimal where the costs of doing business are on a downward sloping curve, such as when economies of scale are pronounced, Nilsson adds.

He cites, for example, the marketing cooperatives that gather and handle agricultural raw materials, especially in the first stages of the processing chain. "Under such conditions, it is always an advantage for all the existing owners/suppliers/members if one new supplier is added and if the existing suppliers increase their volumes," he says. "The fact that the new ones (suppliers) pay small financial contributions for their membership is of less importance than their contribution to volume and thereby to the reduction of average costs."

Professor Nilsson offers the following example to explain the *portfolio choice problem*:

A few years ago, a large Swedish grain and supply cooperative bought a large grain firm in the former East Germany. This doubled the turnover (business volume) of the cooperative. It also turned out to be "an enormous economic failure" for the cooperative, he said, resulting in the firm losing a lot of money.

"But even if the purchase had been a success and resulted in profits, the decision would not have been in the interests of the (Swedish) members," he explains. "Each member has his own set of preferences as to risk levels, capital return levels, etc., and an investment like the German (acquisition) would not be regarded as the most desirable by many members if they had the possibility of making individual decisions.

"One member would have preferred to get the corresponding amount (of the investment) in cash to pay for his children's education; another would rather reduce his debts; still another would like to invest the money on the stock exchange, and so on," he says. "Hence, the purchase of the German firm cannot be a compromise or a synthesis of the interests of the members."

But at this point Professor Nilsson makes an important distinction between strategies for a cooperative's international investment. The portfolio choice problem is real, he says, if the cooperative invested for the purpose of capital returns. "Its investments should have the purpose of promoting the sale and processing of the raw materials delivered by the members," he says. "For the latter type of investments, the portfolio choice problem doesn't apply."

The *horizon problem* concerns the different perspectives from which young and old members see their cooperatives, Nilsson explains. It is difficult for a board or management to set policies suited to the interests of both groups. Young farmers may take on debts to yield benefits on a long-term basis; the older farmers want to get the largest returns possible before they retire.

"Moreover, while young farmers used to take over the farms of their parents, this doesn't happen all that often nowadays," he says. "Now, when a farmer retires, a neighboring farmer often takes over the farm so the membership is not passed on to a son or daughter."

Nilsson suggests later that member involvement can mitigate problems with horizon, just as it can overcome the *decision-maker problem*. According to critics of decision-making within cooperatives, it is difficult to give members "a real say," Nilsson explains. A manager or board may listen to 20, 30, or at the very most, 50 members, but the critics doubt the cooperative decision-makers can listen to 20,000 members. "Listening to members also means you will pay attention to those screaming loudest," he says.

"Finally, there is the *control problem*," Professor Nilsson continues. "The top managers are the ones who are best informed, most often better than the board which has the task of controlling the management. And the members might have difficulty controlling the board," he explains.

Nilsson cites the word of Erik Boettcher, a professor of cooperative business in Germany, who says members have informational problems, motivational problems and organizational problems in controlling boards and managers.(6)

Answering the critics

Problems of this kind, based on the agency theory, are widely heard in Sweden nowadays, Professor Nilsson says. And the critics claim these problems have general validity.

"I do not agree!

"They are applicable only if member involvement is very low, i.e., if the cooperative no longer has a role to play in reducing the transaction costs for its members," he says.

"The theory is based on the presumption that all investments have the purpose of attaining capital returns, (and) it does not take into consideration that investment / ownership can have the purpose of securing trade relations."

Agency theory problems are, thus, limited in Swedish agricultural cooperatives, though examples can be found, he said. Agency theory problems may be more significant with consumer cooperatives around the world.

Nilsson said he studied Coop Austria (Konsum Ostereich) in 1995 when it was being dissolved. Members were "totally ignorant of the cooperative" and the control problem was tremendous, he says. The managers and the board were completely under the control of labor unions that, in turn, ran the firm from the perspective of their own interests. "So, the general manager could buy himself a house that looked like a castle; the labor unions used Coop Austria as a vehicle for their own labor policy; the personnel costs were 30 percent higher compared to the main competitor, etc.

"Evidently, all decision-makers knew that the firm was losing a lot of money and that the end was approaching, but as they all thought, 'Konsum will probably survive during my period in office,' nobody took action," Nilsson said. "This is an expression of the horizon problem (as well)."

Transaction cost theory: the rationale for cooperatives

The rationale for cooperatives is best explained by *transaction cost theory*, says Professor Nilsson. For the purpose of conducting some business, a group invests in assets that would have less value in other uses. As a result, it becomes necessary for the group to protect its "transaction specific investments" from the eventual dishonest behavior of trading partners. In other words, he says, after the group members have made their investments, the market mechanism does not function perfectly for them. They become weak and vulnerable market actors. To protect themselves, then, Nilsson says the group (cooperative) decides it had better own the trading partner.

The existence of cooperatives in various sectors, industries, countries and regions worldwide is well explained by this transaction cost theory, he says. Agricultural production is generally characterized by large investments in physical assets that can hardly be used for anything other than farming, and this production is subject to great uncertainties. Hence, Nilsson says, "we find cooperatives within the agricultural sector in practically all countries all over the world." He cites milk, and the dairy industry, as an extreme case of transaction specific investments and uncertainties; thus, dairy cooperatives have generally higher market shares than other agricultural industries.

Farmers in remote and broadly dispersed regions have a higher risk of being exploited by local or regional monopsonists, he notes. This explains the strength of cooperative businesses in Nordic countries and parts of North America. "With only one or very few buyers of their produce, they are in a weak bargaining position," he says.

So, cooperatives have the task of reducing the transaction costs for their members, i.e., they have roles to play in situations when the market mechanism does not function satisfactorily for a number of economic players. If and when the market mechanism functions again, there is no reason to retain the cooperative business mode – provided that the dissolution of the cooperative does not give rise to the same market failures that prevailed before the cooperative. (7)

Rather than keep cooperatives that are no longer needed as cooperatives, Professor Nilsson suggests the members sell their enterprises and split the sales revenue among themselves. He is critical of consumer cooperatives in several European countries where the retail market functions so well the cooperatives are no longer needed. He suspects the same is true for some agricultural cooperatives in some countries, citing some meat cooperatives in Germany and cooperatives for various industries in France.

The need for cooperatives

Present economic development trends towards concentration and specialization give contradictory signals on the future of cooperatives, says Nilsson. "The farms are getting bigger, but they will still be dwarfs in relation to buyers," he states. Even where farming becomes more geographically concentrated, economies of scale for buyers still won't assure sufficient competition. Furthermore, he adds, as farming and processing techniques become more specialized, the markets are changing character – and that, too, means the actors (farmers and processing firms) will have a limited number of potential trading partners.

Nilsson cites the trends now seen in poultry and pig (pork) production, especially in the United States and parts of Europe. "Evidently, there are strong advantages in strict coordination of the various stages of the value chain, leading to almost full vertical integration," he says. "The entire chain is owned by very large investor-owned firms (IOFs), with their roots, for example, in the feeding business. The farmers' role is only to follow the very specified procedure for raising the chickens or pigs that are owned by the firm. So the farmer is hardly any longer a free businessman.

"Imagine how different it would be if this firm was a cooperative instead of an IOF!" Nilsson adds. **(8)**

There will be a need for cooperation among agricultural producers in the future, Nilsson concludes, but farmers will face great changes in terms of organizational and financial arrangements for their businesses. This is coming, he says, even though it is difficult for many farmers to recognize the great value that cooperatives have for them. They are, he notes, reluctant to integrate their operations with the cooperative – for financing, trading conditions and control – even when it is in their long-term interest.

Defining the cooperative: can it deviate from its origins?

"There are many definitions, short ones and exhaustive ones," Professor Nilsson says. "My concept is:

"...It is a business activity; it is owned by its members; it works in their interest; and it is controlled by them. This is a 'to-the-point' definition and completely in line with the definitions used by American agricultural cooperative researchers," he says.

It its broad enough to include all types of cooperatives, yet is so precise that it can be of help in a lot of theoretical analyses, Nilsson adds. And the definition has its roots in general theory. Using this definition as a starting point, he explains, "one can deduce a workable set of cooperative principles – or should I say that this definition makes other cooperative principles unnecessary. Many other definitions have a pronounced ideological content; and so, they are of no theoretical value – they are more misleading."

Given this definition, Professor Nilsson is wary of a cooperative having outside investors. "... especially if these outsiders get formal power, i.e., voting rights," he says. But without voting rights, he notes such ownership is risky because the interests of the capital owners and the members are not necessarily compatible. Outside capital owners could harm the cooperative by threatening to withdraw their capital; by spreading bad will if they consider themselves as being treated poorly; and if unsatisfied, they can make it difficult for the cooperative to acquire new sources of capital. For those reasons, he adds, "I am even skeptical of letting retired members remain as members, especially if they retain their voting rights."

For these reasons, Professor Nilsson says members should finance the cooperative. If they do not want to invest, this could indicate they do not consider the cooperative's operations to be sufficiently valuable for them, and the cooperative should consider this message before entering the market. But external capital is possible when it comes to investments far ahead in the processing chain, for such assets as plants that manufacture ready-to-eat food products.

A decisive factor is whether the market mechanism functions satisfactorily at the level of the members, he says. The farther one gets forward in the processing chain, the smaller the risk in threatening the individual farmers' investments.

"Collection and the first processing (until the product has reached a nonperishable and standardized form) must be owned fully by the cooperative," Nilsson explains. "The following stage or stages of the processing (adding value to large volumes) could be owned jointly by the cooperative and by individual farmer/members." And processing still farther ahead in the chain, such as operations that are subject to caprices of markets and international competition, risky and capital intensive operations, could be owned with outside capital. And, he adds, it may be just as well if the cooperative is not a player in these later stages.

Differences in agricultural sectors

The cooperative banking sector in Sweden is different than systems found in other countries, Nilsson says. The farmer-owned Rabobank is a major, money center bank in the Netherlands, he points out. "This is something we do not have in Sweden." The Swedish Foreningsbanken tried to become a large, "real bank" in the 1980s, he explains. With foreign loans, the bank management provided non-agricultural financing. But in the early 1990s, when the real estate market collapsed in Sweden and all banks reported major losses, the Federation of Swedish Farmers had to rescue the bank from bankruptcy. (9) The bank has since been transformed into a public stock company with former members becoming shareholders.(10) It remains the major bank for the agricultural sector, including cooperatives, he says. And when it comes to long-term financing of mortgages, the cooperative mortgage bank Hypteksbanken is dominant, he adds.

Regarding other sectors, Professor Nilsson draws comparisons with Dutch agribusiness cooperatives. "Holland is dominating the Swedish market with its horticultural products," he says. "You have good quality, but above all, you have very competitive prices." This follows not only from favorable climatic conditions, but from the Dutch ability to use advantages of scale. While the Dutch "veilings," or auction and marketing cooperatives, have bridged the conflicting interests of its producers, the Swedish horticultural cooperatives are continually reorganizing in response to internal fights, he explains.

"I made the same observations in Austria recently: a market gardener told me that he – located just outside Vienna – could hardly compete on the Viennese market with the flood of cheap products coming from the Netherlands."

Having said that, however, Nilsson adds that he doesn't consider Dutch agribusiness to be all globally oriented. It relies heavily on German markets and neighboring countries. "Denmark has really internationalized agribusiness on a global scale," he says in comparison. "The Danes have a strong position in the United States and many countries in East Asia, including Japan. The explanation might be that Denmark is smaller than the Netherlands. Denmark has only five million inhabitants, but a major agribusiness sector; they simply have to market their products all over the world. And the Danish food industry is considered to be the most dangerous threat to the Swedish producers, with the Dutch as No. 2."

Member involvement

Member involvement is the most valuable asset of a cooperative, insists Professor Nilsson. "If the members consider the cooperative to be important to them, they are willing to finance the company; they want to trade with it; they take part in the control of the cooperative; they are willing to accept the rules of the cooperative and subordinate themselves for the best of the entire membership. But it should be stressed that genuine involvement could not result from propaganda and speeches – it follows from the fact that the cooperatives are the best alternative for the members!"

Simply put, the cooperative must be able to solve the farmers' actual problems, such as remedy market failures and reduce the farmers' transaction costs, he says.

In Sweden, member involvement is generally high. In some cases, especially the dairy industry, about half the members attend their annual district assemblies. The attendance is lower in the grain cooperatives, he says. And for comparison, he notes, "it is next to zero in the consumer cooperatives. The British consumer cooperatives have a member attendance rate of about one member per two thousand!"

Contrary to common belief, Nilsson says member involvement doesn't seem to be related to the size of the membership. There are small cooperatives where member democracy functions badly, and large cooperatives where members "are very alert." The decisive factor is the importance the cooperative has for its members, he says; such as the transaction cost reducing capability of the cooperative.

The Danish meat cooperatives provide a good example of that, he says. The members are very involved. Becoming elected to boards is important. And, as he noted earlier, many Danish farmers are heavily indebted and their cooperative is capable of offering good prices for their animals.

Capital formation

The most urgent problem facing cooperatives worldwide seems to be capital formation. The traditional cooperative model for equity capital is a problem, he says. Most often, cooperatives have a large amount of collective capital (11), which means that earlier generations of members subsidize present members. As part of the profits are set aside as new collective capital, the present members will subsidize future members.

"Most often, the individual capital gets no interest, or low interest rates are paid," he adds, so older members subsidize younger members. Further, he says, the fact that equity capital is cheap to the cooperative means that too much capital is used.

These subsidizations distort market forces, Nilsson says, and they hamper the efficiency of the cooperative business. One remedy might be to pay interest rates to individual members equivalent to market rates. Another measure would be increasing the proportionate share of the members' capital.

"Collective capital is suitable only for the first stage or stages of processing in the value chain," he says. "Collective capital is not suitable for the processing of member products far ahead in the value chain, as those activities are generally characterized by turbulent market needs." For those latter activities, individual member capital or external capital is better. Again, he says, the decisive factor becomes whether the market mechanism functions satisfactorily from the level of the farmers. If it does, he argues, the farmers have no reason to own a cooperative business.(12)

There are reasons for taking a critical look at collective capital, says Nilsson while expanding on the theme. Where the collective capital becomes dominant, the cooperative takes on the character of a foundation. Meanwhile, owning some assets collectively is equivalent to not owning it at all, he says. The involvement of the members is at danger when they do not have much ownership in the cooperative.

Moreover, Nilsson warns that collective capital can become counter-productive by distorting market forces and the operations of the cooperative. The capital can contribute to creating a cash surplus within the cooperative, and this surplus is passed along to the members in the form of higher prices for their delivered raw products. Hence, the prices paid to the members become higher than the market rate, resulting in larger production volumes by the members. Prices subsequently fall when these large volumes reach the market, "and resources have been wasted. A cooperative cannot in the long run deviate significantly from the market price level.

"So, instead of having maximum produce prices as its goal, the cooperative should have a goal to maximize the incomes of its members..."

There is another issue about collective capital that should be examined, Nilsson says, and that is how it creates a "lock-in effect" on the organization. "Suppose that the members' and society's need for some of the business branches of the cooperative becomes reduced or changed so that the firm should be dissolved, sold or at least restructured towards some other business activities," he says. "This becomes difficult if the capital is not mobile as it should be in a well-functioning market economy. This is another argument for collective ownership only in the first stages of the processing chain." (13)

Collective capital: the case in Sweden

As in many countries, a large part of the equity capital in Swedish agricultural cooperatives is represented by collective capital, Nilsson says. It varies from industries and enterprises, often reaching from 80 percent to 90 percent of the total equity capital. But some thirty years ago, the proportion was reversed, he says. There are reasons why this occurred:

"First, the taxation law. If the cooperatives funded their profits collectively rather than forwarding the profits to the members, the total amount of taxes could be minimized; and so they did. This taxation law was, of course, absurd," he explains, noting that the law has been amended in recent years and the cooperatives no longer use collective funding of profits to the same extent.

Secondly, he continues, was the generous former Swedish agricultural policy that was in operation until 1990. "The Federation of Swedish Farmers was so successful in its negotiations with the state that it was not necessary for cooperatives to forward all the (profit) amounts to the farmers. A good share of it could stay within the cooperatives, in the industry-wide federations, and in the Federation of Swedish Farmers," he says.

The result of these past Swedish policies has left the agricultural cooperative sector very wealthy, he says. Equity rates often reach 40 percent to 50 percent (14); and the federated organizations have money to invest in non-member business. "Such investments are perhaps not in accordance with any cooperative theory," he adds, "but those assets may prove valuable when international competition becomes extremely fierce."

Pooling transaction costs

One of the ways Swedish farmers share transaction costs is through a cooperative principle they've coined called "*distance neutrality.*" While it may have fewer consequences in the Netherlands, it does apply to certain cooperative ventures in the United States and Canada. (15) In simple form, Professor Nilsson explains, the cooperative pays the transportation costs no matter where the producer lives.

"This distance neutrality is extremely costly in Sweden due to long distances," he says. "Members who live close to the cooperative's plants are paying for members living far away. There are cases in which collecting the milk from a remote dairy farmer costs more than double the price it yields. I have read about a milk producer living one hundred kilometers from the nearest neighboring dairy farm, and this farmer has just expanded his operations."

Nilsson says he's also heard from a cooperative slaughterhouse (abattoir) who told of receiving a shipment of ten sheep from a member. The transportation costs were higher than the value of the meat. "It is evident from these examples that the principle of distance neutrality has to be revised," he says. "Even though agricultural cooperatives in the competing countries, mainly Denmark and Holland, also apply the same principle, the effects are not the same due to the differences in geography."

Swedish forestry is starting to make some adjustments, he notes. Forest product prices depend on world market prices. "Due to cut-throat competition in this area, the Swedish wood processing cooperatives have been forced to ask transport costs from member forest owners who may have forests hundreds of kilometers away from the sawmill, pulp plant or export harbor." As a consequence, he says, "the distant forests – far from the coast – have lost a good share of their value."

Product and market development

Given the problems, and practices, of cooperatives that separate them from investor owned firms, Professor Nilsson was asked to comment on the cooperatives' abilities to compete in making consumer products.

Dr. Karin Tollin addressed the issue in her dissertation, Nilsson says, in which she concluded that Swedish cooperatives "think less in commercial terms, have more centralized power, and need a long time to adapt to consumer demand."(16) But in separate research, Dr. Harry Nystrom at Uppsala University made a comparative study on product development within the Swedish dairy sector.(17) "He found that cooperatives are somewhat ahead of the IOFs. This different conclusion can perhaps be explained by the fact the dairy industry is dominated by one very large and internationally oriented cooperative, Arla."

A Danish researcher, Villy Sogaard, has also contributed to the discussion, Nilsson says. In his 1994 book, Sogaard states that Danish slaughterhouses can produce high quality commodities in bulk volume thanks to their cooperative character.(18) He's not sure they could achieve this as IOF companies. He cites, for example, the cooperatives working to develop specific types of pigs to yield more expensive meats to meet consumer demands.

Choice of products

A cooperative shouldn't invest money for the sole sake of getting a return on investment, Nilsson insists. An agricultural cooperative should work in the interests of its members. It should market its farmers' products, in a more or less processed form, with the objective of supporting its members' economy through good prices or other economic benefits. "The farmer is a member as a farmer; not as an investor. If the cooperative has excess cash, the members could invest this money individually in accordance with their own conditions."

Nilsson said there are Swedish examples where cooperatives have made investments that have no connection to the members' business. He cites a dairy cooperative that bought a mineral water plant that doesn't promote the sale of milk products. "An investor-owned firm could have diversified its business like this, but a cooperative should not diversify outside the realm of its members," he insists. "The diversification which is needed in agriculture should take place at the farm level, just like the investor diversifies by spreading his investments on the stock exchange."

Nilsson adds that this doesn't preclude a cooperative from working with products originating from other suppliers. Often, he notes, members products can be sold at higher prices and in larger volumes to new markets if the cooperative combines products from different origins. "One example is the combined butter-margarine spread, offered by many dairy cooperatives. Another is the sale of juices, whereby the dairy cooperative can make use of free capacity in the production plant, storage houses and truck fleets, since the production and distribution techniques are the same as for milk.

What is important, however, is that the outside products supplement member products in one of several stages of the production-distribution marketing chain, he says. Therefore, supplementing and substituting are not conflicting practices, he adds, and the substitutes may include some products that increase the value of the cooperatives' portfolio for retailers and consumers.

Evaluating cooperative success

Measuring the success or failure of a cooperative must start with defining the original goal of the organization, says the Swedish cooperative expert. He notes that Axel Bansch, (19) in his dissertation, says the only true measure of success is the rate of growth or decline in membership and turnover (gross revenues). "This is relevant, but it can hardly be sufficient," observes Nilsson.

If a cooperative was established to solve a group of members' problems with a badly functioning market, he says, the fact members are leaving the cooperative may signal its own success. The market failure has been erased or corrected, and the members may not need the cooperative any longer. This observation dates back to 1937, he notes, when Henry Bakken and Marvin Schaars referred to cooperatives as "self-liquidating corporations. Their success may cause their destruction." (20)

But moving onward in time, Nilsson adds that second generation members of a cooperative may underestimate the value of their organization since they have never experienced a market without their cooperative business.

Cooperative organizational structures

"Cooperation between cooperatives" is often considered to be a characteristic of cooperative business. The International Cooperative Alliance considers this to be a principle to be followed by all member organizations. For his part, Professor Nilsson takes a skeptical view.

"Like all other business organizations, cooperatives should collaborate with the best partners, not necessarily with other cooperatives," he says. There are theoretical reasons why other cooperatives may be better partners than IOFs, such as similar cultures and values. But these arguments are ambiguous, he adds. "Furthermore, it is difficult to attain an equal power balance in collaborative arrangements, with the effect that the stronger partner could come to eat the weaker partner."

Nilsson cites the Danish dairy cooperative MD Foods as an example. During its growth, MD made numerous alliances with smaller dairies. The result was the latter weakened their financial status to the point where MD was able to buy them cheaply or assimilate them easily, he says.

Another example is Skanemejerier, in the southernmost province of Sweden. It is a small dairy cooperative geographically squeezed between two giants – Arla (with 68 percent of the Swedish milk volume) and MD Foods. Swedish competition authorities would not permit a merger or collaboration with Arla, he explains, and an alliance with MD would make a skewed power relationship. As a result, Skanemejerier formed an alliance with Klovermaelk, Denmark's second largest dairy cooperative. They now market each other's products and jointly own a successful dairy firm in Poland.

Meanwhile, Nilsson says, Klovermaelk has started to collaborate closely with MD Foods ("the Danish competition law is extremely liberal"). "As a consequence, Skanemejerier's long-run survival as an independent cooperative is no longer certain," he says. "MD Foods is very much stronger than both Klovermaelk and Skanemejerier, not only financially but (also) in terms of attractive products, marketing skills and distribution network."

Cooperation between cooperatives has traditionally taken place within federations, he adds, despite some inherently weak attributes to the federated organization form. Power relationships are usually unclear, authority is loosely defined; it is often difficult to distinguish between orders and advice. The federated organization seems to work well when there is a large number of member organizations of about equal size and strength, he says, and when the central organization can be forced to do what it was formed to do – as a servant of its members.

"In today's cooperative world, a network of jointly owned subsidiaries is a more promising way of inter-cooperative cooperation – and also with non-cooperative firms as partners," states Nilsson. "Thereby, the locus of power is better defined, the authority relations becomes evident, and the tasks of the organization become more clearly stated," he says. "After all, we must realize that the partners collaborate to further their own interests and so, there are always risks for conflict."

Villy Sogaard, the Danish researcher, has shown that federated organizations tend to fall over if they are somewhat imbalanced, Nilsson recalls.(21) "Then the process of 'the big fish eating the smaller fish but is eaten by a still bigger fish' comes into operation," he explains in pointing at three patterns of events:

"*First*, the federated organization could eat the member cooperatives, possibly after the struggle between the members organizations cause them to lose power.

"*Second*, the biggest one could eat the others so that it finally assimilates the federation.

"*Third*, the federation might be dissolved altogether after the biggest has eaten some of the smaller member organizations.

"There are many observations to support Dr. Sogaard's thesis that federations are an unstable type of organization in the long run," Nilsson says.

Mergers

Another organizational tool for obtaining economies of scale is merger, Professor Nilsson, noting that there have been several waves of mergers over the decade. This process isn't over, he adds, predicting that there will be more domestic mergers all over Europe before cooperatives enter international mergers.

One barrier to international merger will be national competition authorities that fear amalgamated cooperatives may abuse their market power, he forecasts. "Even though open membership cooperatives with no control of farm production decisions have a high threshold before they can influence market prices, it must be acknowledged that this kind of problem might arise, as explained by Professor Richard Sexton of California," Nilsson adds.(22)

Another barrier to international cooperative mergers is related to membership, Professor Nilsson continues. Increasing heterogeneity of the membership might give rise to conflicting demands and communications problems, he says, and the still more complex organization would make it more difficult for members to control boards and management.

As a solution to those problems, Professor Nilsson suggests the cooperative decentralize its membership and, as far as possible, its business operations. The latter could be done by creating regional "profit centers" under the control of local or regional memberships.(23) "This model is now suggested in connection with a proposed merger among some Swedish grain and supply cooperatives which would result in one cooperative covering more than half the country's arable land," he says.

Dissolving cooperatives

Finally, any discussion on the future of cooperatives must explore issues of dissolvement. And, insists Professor Nilsson, "It must be possible to dissolve a cooperative in the best interest of the members."

Two examples in Northern Europe explain the reasons why, he says.

Denmark had two sugar processing companies. One is Danisco, a large IOF, and the other is a small, farmer-owned cooperative, Nykobings Sukkerfabrik. "Danisco wanted to take over the cooperative, but generally, that is difficult since membership of a cooperative is not negotiable," Nilsson recalls. So, in 1990, Danisco offered a large sum to cooperative members willing to dissolve their company. "It has been said that all farmers became millionaires, in Danish currency," adding that as long as the European Union guarantees the price of sugar beets, the farmers probably didn't need a cooperative.

Another major development was pending at the time of this interview in October, 1995. It involves Absolut Vodka, the No. 1 selling premium vodka brand in the United States and a popular distilled spirit throughout the industrialized world, which was jointly owned by the Swedish government and a potato growers cooperative. Nilsson said that modern technology has converted the distillery so vodka is now made from wheat, not the members' potatoes. "Therefore, the potato cooperative's members no longer have interest in the distillery as suppliers," he explained. The government realized it would be easier and more profitable to sell the entire enterprise, not just its ownership stake, so it was negotiating to buy out the farmers.

"There again, the member-farmers will get a considerable amount of money," predicts Nilsson. "Nobody doubts that the cooperative will sell its shares, and so it will be dissolved."

Chapter Footnotes

1. The interview with Professor Nilsson was conducted in Copenhagen on Oct. 5, 1995. His depiction of the cooperative environment in Sweden seemed harsh to the American editor, Egerstrom, whose ancestors immigrated from Sweden in the 1880s. In March, 1996, however, three members of the Commission on Competition in Trade with Agricultural Commodities and Food, the Swedish Ministry of Industry and Commerce, visited with Egerstrom on a fact gathering tour of the United States. Following that meeting, Egerstrom is inclined to mix the following agrarian metaphors: "There are no 'sacred cows' left in Sweden, cooperative or not;" and, "It is possible to kill the goose that laid the 'golden egg'."

2. The Swedish intelligensia being sent to other countries, as those mentioned in Footnote 1, are likely to study ways to put Swedish cooperative laws in harmony with other national cooperative codes. That is likely, the editors assume, if the Swedes are serious about positioning their agricultural economy competitively with other European nations.

3. Tax treatment of patronage refunds and interest earned by outside investors – where allowed – is likely to vary greatly from one country to the next. However, it should be noted for American and Canadian readers, that the 'one member, one vote' principle that doesn't account for equity ownership may preclude the "closed membership," New Generation Cooperatives as described by Cook and Egerstrom.

4. This condition varies from country to country, depending on national laws on cooperatives – the editors.

5. This is the case with the closed membership, New Generation Cooperatives in North America.

6. Boettcher, Erik (1980): _Die Genossenschaft in der Marktwirtschaft_. Tubingen: JCB Mohr (Paul Siebeck).

7. This point may have special relevance in North America. Farmers, located far distances from the major marketing cooperatives' headquarters, may not always recognize the transaction cost services provided by their organizations. But as they take stock of those services, they might ask: "If not Agway, Cenex, Countrymark, Farmland, Gold

Kist, Growmark, Harvest States, Land O'Lakes, Manitoba Wheat Pool, Saskatchewan Wheat Pool; then who?"

8. About one-fourth of all pigs raised in America are now controlled by vertically integrated agribusiness and meat companies. It does appear that this growing concentration has altered, if not voided, the historic cycles of pig production (Purdue University and Iowa State University research.) Some American farmers have responded to this rapid takeover of the U.S. pork industry by banding together and forming New Generation Cooperatives to achieve the large agribusiness firms' economies of scale in using technologies, genetics, nutrition and health and safety practices. (See: Cook, Egerstrom.)

(9) The Federation of Swedish Farmers may be compared to the Nationale Cooperetieve Raad (NCR) in the Netherlands or the National Council of Farmer Cooperatives (NCFC) in the United States.

(10) For the Dutch: a public limited company (*Naamlose Vennootschap*).

(11) Within cooperative business, this is known as "capital in the dead hand" (*kapitaal in de dode hand*).

(12) Professor Nilsson's point is well taken. It occurs to the editors, however, that American economists and cooperative leaders may want to study this concept more closely in regards the New Generation Cooperatives. It may well be that the increasing takeover of poultry and pig production by a small number of vertically integrated food companies represents a classic example of market failure; thus, farmers may have historical economic justifications for seeking income from higher rungs on the food ladder through pooling production resources in their new cooperatives. This question deserves serious academic study.

(13) The seriousness of restrictions on the distribution, mobility and use of collective capital varies from country to country, depending on national cooperative business laws.

(14) The Dutch call this equity rate "*soliditeit*;" Americans might call this their "capital base."

(15) The U.S. grain industry greatly eliminates "distance neutrality" issues through the process of "basis points," or the transaction costs applied to grain prices to move the grain into a market position. A question remains, however, if "distance neutrality" will become an issue in the American dairy industry with federal dairy policies distorting the location of dairy production.

(16) Tollin, Karin (1990): *Konsumentbilder i marknadsforingen av livsmedel. En studie om marknadsforingens kontext inom svensk*

lantbrukskooperative livsmedelsindustri (Consumer Images in Food Marketing: A Study about the Context of Marketing within the Swedish Agricultural Cooperative Food Industry). Stockholm: University of Stockholm.

(17) Nystrom, Harry & Bo Edvardsson (1982): *Product Innovation in Food Processing – A Swedish Survey.* R & D Management, Vol. 12, No. 2..

(18) Sogaard, Villy (1994): *Farmers, Cooperatives, New Food Products.* Aarhus: MAPP (Aarhus School of Business).

(19) Bansch, Axel (1983): *Operationalisierung des Unternehmenszieles Mitgliederforderung.* Gottingen: Vanderhoeck & Ruprecht.

(20) Bakken, Henry & Marvin Schaars (1937) The Economics of Cooperative Marketing. New York: McGraw-Hill.

(21) Sogaard, Villy (1990): *Spildt Maelk? En analyse af konkurrence, samarbejde og solidaritet mellem landbrugets andelsvirksomheder* (Spilled Milk? An Analysis of Competition, Collaboration and Solidarity Among Agricultural Cooperatives). Esbjerg: South Jutland University Press.

(22) Sexton, Richard (1990): "*Imperfect Competition in Agricultural Markets and the Role of Cooperatives: A Spatial Analysis,*" American Journal of Agricultural Economics. Vol. 72, No. 3; and,

Sexton, Richard (1995): *Analysis and Evaluation of Competition Policies Affecting Agricultural Cooperatives With Special Reference to the Swedish Economy.* Report for the Swedish Government Commission on the application of the competition rules.

(23) This form of shared, federated operations is largely in place at Harvest States Cooperatives in the Northern U.S. states, notes veteran cooperative official and writer Jim Erickson. Harvest States has regionalized its operations, which not only allows but encourages local cooperatives to operate as separate "profit centers."

PROFESSOR DR. WERNER GROSSKOPF

A VIEW FROM GERMANY

Professor Dr. Werner Grosskopf, 54, was born in Aken, Germany, and graduated in Agricultural Economics at the University of Gottingen where he continued to do research for several years. He completed his graduate studies at the University of California at Berkeley (USA) in 1971, after which he lectured for a short period of time at the University of Hamburg. He was appointed professor at the University of Gottingen in 1973, and in 1981, he moved south to the University of Hohenheim at Stuttgart, where he continues to lecture.

Professor Grosskopf is also director of the Institute of Agricultural Markets and the Research Center of the Cooperative Movement. Recent research of the institute has focused on the influence of the cooperative member, quality of products, the optimal size of cooperatives, and how best to deal with mergers. Besides research, the institute provides advisory services to individual cooperatives.

HOW FARMER-DIRECTORS CAN INFLUENCE STRATEGIC DECISION-MAKING
By Professor Dr. Gert van Dijk and Dr. Jan Werts

In the early 1900s, dairy farmers in the western regions of Germany needed to come to grips with their future and that of their dairy cooperative. What they chose to do, and why they did it, sheds light on some unique problems for cooperatives in Germany. And in a much broader sense, the German farmers raise questions about governance and capital formation that will need to be answered in every nation.

Let's have Professor Werner Grosskopf of the University of Hohenheim (Stuttgart, Germany) explain it:

"There was the investor-owned Müller Dairy Group, with interests in Ireland and the new German (Eastern) states. Danone was also interested, and so was Campina Melkunie, of course. One alternative was a 'buy-out' of Südmilch by its farmer-owners. At the time this range of options caused an animated debate within the region. Everyone joined in, from farmers' associations to the minister of agriculture."

After the debate ended, the Dutch cooperative Campina Melkunie took over the German cooperative Südmilch in 1993. In reviewing the options that were available, Professor Grosskopf notes that Campina Melkunie won when German farmers did not succeed in taking over their cooperative. Directors and farmers looked into the matter thoroughly. It was not possible for them to acquire the 25 % of shares needed; the farmers were only able to raise financing for a few percent. Members of Campina Melkunie were able to finance the takeover, although they had to dig deep into their pockets to do so. "Their willingness was influenced by the large amount of 'know-how' in Südmilch and its basically solid condition," Grosskopf says.

The Südmilch episode made it clear that German farmers and horticultural producers have little or no capital to spare for investment in their cooperatives. They are only prepared to invest to a limited extent, but not every three years or so as needs arise. "In this case, you need to tap other sources," says Grosskopf. "You can have a cooperative built on outside capital, supplied by members of special status: in addition to farmer-members, you have those who only supply capital." This is no humbug in Professor Grosskopf's opinion, but a realistic option – perhaps even a necessity.

"I expect there to be three categories of relationships in cooperatives in the future. First, there will be people that only make use of it; they are not owners, only users. Second, there will be members in the classical sense. Third, there will be the new, financial participants. The European Union is considering adopting these three categories as the basis of the structure of future cooperatives in the Union. This sort of investment we would term 'advantages', since certain participants, i.e. those holding preferential shares, would have special rights in the distribution of profits as is found elsewhere in business.(1)

This last group has become one of the most important suppliers of capital to the cooperative banks in Germany, and this has spread to other cooperatives. For example, in some dairy cooperatives holders of preferential shares receive extra payments related to the cooperative's trading results, over and above their minimum guaranteed payments. These preferential shares would have a term of twelve to twenty years, he says.

Supervision of management and the board of directors

Although it is sometimes very difficult for farmers to supply the increasing amounts of capital needed, that may not be the greatest challenge facing cooperatives, adds Professor Grosskopf. That challenge is, in fact, the issue of their governance. Essentially, the supervision of strategic, and thus far-reaching, decisions will be crucial to the future of cooperatives. "For example, should we as a cooperative take over another firm? If so, should we restrict our takeovers to firms within our own country, or are, in general, takeovers within Europe all right? Would we prefer to take over French or Spanish firms, or even Polish ones? Such strategic decisions affect the viability of a cooperative firm. It was lack of supervision, pure and simple, that led to Südmilch's problems. If, in simplistic terms, management is no good, then things are bound to go wrong; we've seen it happen with other cooperatives. Things go wrong, too, when management sees itself as occupying one camp and members and directors another."

This problem is dealt with in what economists, political scientists and business professors call the agency theory. It is common in all large societies. In the case of cooperatives, the theory indicates that members and even the board of directors are not able to judge the performance of management adequately, be it good or bad. Moreover, it is usually not possible to replace management when it is performing badly. Conversely, an excellent management that sees a board of directors, or individuals on the board, performing badly will find it difficult to intervene and replace the offending directors because of the risks such a step will create for its own managerial position. This is an important issue in the running of a cooperative.(2)

"Another problem is that directors and managers in many cooperatives have permanent appointments.(3) In business they would be given a contract for, say, five years, and its renewal would be a matter for discussion," Grosskopf says. "If a director on permanent employment does well, there is no problem. However, if after a while it appears you have appointed the wrong person to the job, you do have a problem. The same is, by the way, true of board appointments. Generally, directors sit on boards for far too long. They should be appointed for limited terms, so as to make room for others from time to time. This is also true for supervisory boards," he adds. "Not only farmers, but also representatives of local authorities sit on these boards; members should be replaced every twelve years or so." (4)

Generally speaking, Grosskopf considers it would be an improvement if some board members of the larger cooperatives were drawn from outside the 'cooperative world'.

Advisory boards

Is this, perhaps, too much of an ideal picture – too unrealistic?

"What is important is that farmer-directors are really able (and not just in theory) to influence strategic decision-making," says the German professor. "Perhaps it is asking too much that completely independent experts from outside the cooperative be incorporated in the board of directors. That's why I suggest that an advisory board, comprising several independent specialists, be created. They would meet two to three times a year to review the board of directors' plans and the firm's financial results. ... Find out how they view things; get their opinion on this and that; make use of their specialist knowledge," he says. "Such a board should be consulted every time management intends to make important investments or other decisions with far-reaching consequences. The independent advice of such a board would give farmers and horticultural producers, as well as directors, a clearer picture of such plans."

Management could also count on their critical assessment, Grosskopf continues. This would give farmers and horticultural producers a solid basis from which to direct the running of a large cooperative. "That is none too soon, because – let's face it – an ordinary farmer-director, what we call in Germany a 'token member', however prudent, is not able to judge whether an investment of, say, NLG 200 million (US $130 million), is necessary. I admit there are a few who can do so; but then you run the risk that because of their skill they will dominate the board, or management, or both."

In Grosskopf's opinion, membership of such an advisory board would be a prestige appointment. Because of the high demands made of its members; it would be no token job. "Advisors should be paid. Not excessively, but enough to make it clear that effort and sound advice are expected. Their advice to the board of directors should be put in writing. It is in everybody's interest that the board of directors, the management and the advisory board are able, after sufficient reflection, to conclude whether a certain project should proceed or not."

Governance in this form has more credibility than that by the classical method, whereby 10-15 board members meet a few time each year and only see each other otherwise at social gatherings and the annual dinner, Grosskopf says. "That style of governance has already cost Germany too much money. Remember Südmilch. There, management was free to do as it pleased, and farmer-directors were unable to correct them," he says.

Professor Grosskopf has the idea that the election process of farmer-directors is less democratic in Germany than in other developed countries. Regardless, he adds, "You should be continually aware of the difference between the day to day running of the cooperative, which is a management task, and the strategic management of the cooperative, which is the responsibility of the board of directors. This latter responsibility was even incorporated into German cooperative law some 20 years ago."

Profitable privately-owned firms vs. cooperative firms

There is a popular assumption that stock-exchange-listed public limited companies (PLCs) are more competitive that cooperative firms. The statistics do not bear this out, however. The profitability of such industries as dairying, meat or fruit is better than that of exchange-listed PLCs. It should also be taken into account that cooperatives concentrate on more than profit alone.

In the dairy industry in Germany, Grosskopf distinguishes three types of cooperative firms: "First, there are the large cooperatives, such as Ulzena, Nordmilch and Bavarian Union Milch (even though they are smaller than the Dutch cooperatives). Second, there are the somewhat smaller cooperatives, many with very good products, that sometimes have problems with their finances, and so, too, with their continuity. They are not aggressive traders and as a result they often end up selling their produce to price-cutters. Third, there are privately-owned dairy firms, such as Müller Milch, Zott, Bauer, Meggele, Ehrmann and Weihenstephan. They buy the exact amount of milk they need to make their sophisticated products, such as fine yogurts, desserts and other profitable products. They don't produce in bulk."

These firms are very profitable; the larger cooperatives are less so, and the smaller cooperatives the least, he continues. None of the cooperatives is able to build up sufficient financial reserves. The cooperatives that produce in bulk (butter, milk powder) earn little, he says. One of their main functions is to 'clean up' the market. "You often see such cooperatives operating at marginal levels, and at other moments, competing fiercely with each other, sometimes by not writing off enough."

Recently, the German association of cooperatives began discussing whether it makes more sense in the long run to consolidate the 40-50 national cooperative firms into a smaller number of larger firms. This fragmentation denied German cooperatives the capability of making a serious bid for Südmilch. This weak structure was also the reason why, Grosskopf emphasizes, the large German cooperative Ulzena was forced to contract the sale of its cheese out to Campina Melkunie. "I think that this is the start of internationalization in cooperative enterprise. I wouldn't be surprised if the next step is a takeover of Ulzena by Campina Melkunie. Elsewhere, in the insurance sector, for example, this sort of cooperation is the forerunner of a takeover at a later stage."

Internationalization: necessary but dangerous

Grosskopf is philosophical about the future internationalization of the cooperative. He considers two developments possible: the birth of a European cooperative, which farmers and horticultural producers can join directly; or the creation of a holding company on a European scale, with national or large regional cooperatives as members. The members of the latter would be major cooperatives and the holding would be comparable with a PLC listed on the stock exchanges. The holding company would acquire capital while the cooperatives would remain cooperatives in their own right, with their own institutional and hierarchical structures. At some point the holding would have to make decisions about how and where to invest, but it would be run under the supervision of the member cooperatives. Each member cooperative would have a say proportional to its participation in the total capital formation in the holding. Although the holding may acquire capital from sources other than the cooperatives, for example via preferential shares, the goals of the member cooperatives within their own cooperatives would remain unaffected.

Grosskopf prefers this option to the 'EU cooperative'. The cooperative statutes of the European Union place too much emphasis on social aspects so it is unlikely, given the different circumstances of members, that a typical business-oriented cooperative would evolve.(5)

But in Grosskopf's opinion, there are no alternatives. It is as unavoidable as internationalization.

"In Europe (including the Eastern Europe of the future), the USA, Canada – everywhere, in fact – agribusiness is internationalizing. What's important for farmers and horticultural producers is that they maintain their claim on the international markets, both for sales and purchasing," he says. "It is not unthinkable that poorly performing cooperatives will be taken over in the future by, for example, Nestlé, Danone or Unilever, after which certain groups of farmers may be told that the new owner is no longer interested in their milk in spite of the supply contract they had with the cooperative."

Internationalization is also essential if you are to have access to the large buyers, with their more profitable range of products, Grosskopf adds. Finally, internationalization can enable farmers and horticultural producers to develop the strength (countervailing power) needed to compete more effectively.

"To do all of this, a cooperative must have access to sufficient capital, i.e. financial reserves," he explains. This means that cooperatives may need to pay their members lower prices for raw produce (e.g. milk, meat) for several years running, or that members will have to pay a little more for goods and services such as artificial fertilizer or insurance. "Internationalization also means bearing greater risk; you must be prepared for the eventuality that you may lose money or worse ... go bankrupt. Yet another reason for me to repeat that member-directors must ensure they are supported by a system that supplies relevant, reliable information and that reviews plans and monitors performance along the lines I have already described," says Grosskopf.

He refers to recent research done by his faculty into the background of cooperative banks that have been unprofitable in the past. "Of the 120 cooperative banks we analyzed, 90% ran into problems because of mismanagement relative to speculation in, for example, oil, soya, and even real estate. In nearly every case the board of directors, comprised of ordinary unpaid members, was kept completely in the dark about the transactions; they were there just for the form," he says.

"I'm not at all surprised," he comments. "Every expert knows that management can present the cooperative's accounts in such a way that they won't draw attention to risky investments."

The risk of this happening is greater with internationalization, warns Grosskopf. "A livestock holder from, say, Brabant or North Holland (regions in the Netherlands) may, with good common sense, be able to follow events in Campina Melkunie, for example. It is another thing, however, to judge the investments made in Südmilch, even after two days of asking questions at its head office in Stuttgart. Another problem with internationalization is that it will be difficult, in practice, to effectively integrate farmers and horticultural producers from various countries in one board of directors. I'm all for internationalization, but here you have reached the limits," according to Professor Grosskopf. Internationalization is a necessity for cooperatives, but it is also a danger.

Playing doubles with Steffi Graf ...

Given all this, the question arises as to whether a farmer starting out with 100 cows is better off as a member of a cooperative or just supplying milk to privately-owned firms such as Nutricia or Danone.

"Let's assume this farmer pays DEM 5000 for his membership," says Grosskopf. "One of his first questions will be, 'What is the return?' The answer to which is, 'Not much, because we badly need that capital to process and market your milk.' His next question is likely to be, 'Do I get a say in the decision-making?' Again, if people are honest, he will be told, 'No, because as an individual dairy farmer you are unable to judge whether we, as a cooperative firm, are doing the right thing by contracting Steffi Graff as a marketing symbol.'"

Nevertheless, if Grosskopf was a young farmer he would still join a cooperative, he says, "Because a cooperative has some influence in the market while the alternative is to be forever on your own."

Joint European Union holding

Professor Grosskopf offers a deeper look at the structure of cooperatives in the European Union and the model of the previously mentioned cooperative holding form. He refers to a model in which cooperatives that specialize in primary produce (e.g. milk, sugar, meat), in particular, are associated in a joint holding company. To him, this option is preferable to a huge, Europe-wide cooperative because it offers more flexibility and allows individual member cooperatives to retain their independence to a large degree. The holding could invest in privately-owned firms that produce more profitable, finely-made products that are related to the raw produce of the member cooperatives.

"Südzucker, a (German) sugar cooperative, for example, once began acquiring 5 % of shares of companies producing a diverse range of products, ranging from biscuits to ice cream. Their aim was to gain insight into these branches. If a particular firm did well, Südzucker would acquire 25 % of shares, this time with the aim of influencing the decision-making. Later on, they might decide to become the majority shareholder. In this way, Südzucker was successful in acquiring various firms throughout Europe," he says.

A firm like this, which operates strategically, is attractive to private investors, he notes further. A similar system of national cooperatives operating in a joint international holding, with its own framework and rules and regulations, is preferable to an EU cooperative whose juridical form would be less flexible. "An EU holding based on shares held by national cooperatives reminds me of the system with which Japanese car makers have conquered the automobile markets of the world.

"Here, I must stress that in every sector except banking, our cooperatives are still too small to carry out anything like this. First, a high level of concentration of cooperatives is necessary. In this respect, many West German cooperatives have invested heavily in the new German states since reunification in 1989. Generally, the results have been good, although there are problems in some sectors, such as meat."

Let's assume the management of a factory that is owned by the cooperative holding makes expensive milk-based desserts. What happens if they can buy their milk cheaper from dairy farmers who are not members of a cooperative? Should the management be allowed to do so?

"Management should not have that sort of mandate," answers Grosskopf. "In my opinion, that is a joint decision to be made by the cooperatives in the holding. They would have to balance the divergent interests. Just as they would have to do so, in my opinion, if a particular group of farmers wanted to join the cooperative. If it is in the interests of the members to withhold membership, they may do so. This is quite legal. Just as they may say that only dairy farmers with at least 50 cows are eligible to join the cooperative."

In every cooperative, says Grosskopf, there are three essential conditions: economic advantage for members; influence of members on decision-making; and participation in capital formation by members. Once these are forgotten, the cooperative really does not exist, he says. In contrast, it is possible for a cooperative to do 90% of its business with non-members. "As long as these three conditions are met, it still remains a cooperative – albeit just an investment cooperative," chuckles Grosskopf.

Cooperatives have a future

Agricultural policies affect markets. The recent GATT talks, the MacSharry proposal in the EU, and the future entry of Eastern European countries into the EU have all brought pressure to bear on the system of price support. The question arises whether agricultural cooperatives should attempt to compensate for the drying up of financial support from 'Brussels'.

Werner Grosskopf: "It is clear to me that within the European Union, industry – including agribusiness – has placed its hopes on Eastern Europe as the sales market of the future; EU markets are 'saturated'. That is why, of course, captains of industry are busy behind the scenes pressuring politicians to expand the European Union within a period of five to eight years.

For agriculture this means that relatively high prices for milk, meat, sugar, wine, etc., are a thing of the past. As with prices in the grain sector, these commodity prices will fall to the level of the world market. If this is not enough for farmers to continue on, then their national governments – not the EU – will have to make up the short-fall (if they are prepared to do so). "My countryman, Professor Stefan Tangermann, who has been saying this for years, is right. This is the only way agriculture in the EU can export to the growing markets of Eastern Europe.

"It also appears that Mrs. Thatcher was right after all," jokes Dr. Grosskopf. "This means that cooperatives have to think and operate in European terms. Eastern Europe lays open for agribusiness, too; my contacts in, for example, Poland and Hungary confirm this. Here, as elsewhere, the old saying 'first come, first served' should be heeded."

Cooperatives: the *haute hybrid*

Cooperatives may actually have some inherent strengths for thinking pan-Europe and exploring new opportunities. And one of these strengths can be the cooperative organizational structure. Grosskopf points out that "according to the newest theories of organization, the hierarchical firm run by management from the head office is out. This sort of company has had its day. Remarkably, the characteristics that can be found in the theoretical foundations of the cooperative, with its hybrid structure, make it quite compatible with this development."

Cooperatives have existed for 150 years already on the basis of the now popular subsidiary principle: "what *can* be done locally, *should* be done locally," Grosskopf adds. That's why he expects large cooperatives in the future will have small head offices, particularly as far as services go. "Information and communication allow, for example, bank customers and clients of insurance companies to do most of their business from home via a computer," he says. "Only a few remaining matters need be settled at a regional branch office."

"Next, you hear a lot about total quality management these days, i.e. the continual monitoring and improvement of the quality of the goods and services you are offering," he continues. "I think that this is a typical characteristic of cooperatives since their primary goal is not profit but serving their members as best they can. Finally, there is the present trend towards companies offering a complete range of goods and services. You can see this even in areas where government is withdrawing, such as social services, and (also) in the software industry; cooperatives will move in this way too."

Divisions

The cooperative structure contains more than inherent advantages. It also holds threats for the organization. Professor Grosskopf doesn't have to think for a moment to cite a major one: "the divide between management and members.

"The latter often have too little influence," he says. "Here in Germany, shareholders have, in my opinion, more say in cooperatives than the members.(6) I see it all around me every day.

"This means that management – managers – must learn to think cooperatively and be really interested in the cooperative nature of their firms. I honestly wonder whether, through training, it is possible to become a *Homo cooperativus* or whether you just have to have it in you from the very beginning," Grosskopf adds. "If we only concentrate on management or technical skills in job selection, and not cooperative qualities, it is unlikely that members will have a real role to play in their cooperatives in 20 to 30 years time. It is possible in extreme situations that a limited group of member-owners of, say, a cooperative bank, will want to divide up their assets. The German *Handelsblatt* recently reported that in German banks alone there are DEM 20 million 'without owners'. Farmers and horticultural producers could, if their influence counts for nothing, demand the sale and liquidation of their assets and then go about dividing up the spoils."

Taboos

The question naturally arises as to whether these are matters that can be discussed in cooperatives. Although the question is unexpected, Professor Grosskopf lists several taboos.

"One is the question of whether cooperatives need real members. Isn't it the case that management has dominated affairs for so long now? Every so often, the question is asked jokingly in management circles, 'What are we going to do about our members?' 'Do you need them for financing your operations?' is the reply. 'No,' is the answer. 'What about for decision-making?' Again, 'no' is the rejoinder, once more in a jocular tone, because elsewhere the topic is taboo."

Another taboo cited by Grosskopf concerns members who leave the cooperative after years of participation. Do they have a right to payment according to the real value of their shares, instead of the practice of just paying out the amount they paid into the cooperative? Yet another taboo is the issue of why members of a cooperative bank don't receive higher interest payments. "A few of the smaller cooperative banks have begun to do so, by the way," he adds.

Buy from your neighbors

Though much attention is given to readying cooperatives for international markets, Professor Grosskopf sees trends and strengths for cooperatives in their own backyards. CMA, the German agri-marketing service, has a budget of DEM 120 million, he notes. In addition, each German state has a budget of DEM 3-15 million available, which makes a tidy sum of approximately DEM 150 million to be spent annually on advertising German agricultural products.

Perhaps even more important to 'mammoth' exporters such as the Netherlands and Denmark, these successful advertising campaigns point out to the public that agricultural products from the region, preferably from small, family-owned firms, are tastier, healthier and fresher, he says. The point is also driven home that trucks don't have to travel hundreds of kilometers to deliver the products, thus benefiting the environment.

"'Buy from your neighbors' is the winning slogan," says Grosskopf. Three important states, Bavaria, Saxony and Baden-Württemberg, are setting up mass-media campaigns to point out to the public that local agricultural produce, biodynamic or otherwise, is healthier. "The often mediocre image of the Dutch tomato, which comes from greenhouses far away, is a liability for Dutch agribusiness. German farmers and horticultural producers are making good use of the trend. There are even road maps available that indicate exactly where you can buy local agricultural products on the farm itself. Our beer brewers are also beginning to promote 'beer brewed from hops and barley from your region'. You can see something similar in the meat sector. This is an unmistakable, tremendous development that is unfavorable for exporting countries," he says.

This trend connects with the enormous popularity of the Green Party amongst young people in Germany, Grosskopf continues. There is a similar growing preference for regional produce in France and Italy. International companies such as Nestlé have jumped on the bandwagon by orienting their production to all sorts of regional foodstuffs. "This is simply because the public thinks your 'own' produce is healthier."

For cooperatives that are regionally based and whose marketing is regionally oriented, the ecological approach is important. "I think," says Grosskopf, "that Germany is leading in this. Look at the Green party. Their size has grown election after election. The ecological movement appears to be very popular, particularly amongst the younger generation. That's why the idea has been promoted that food produced in Germany is better than imported food, irrespective of where it comes from. Besides, the Greens expect transport costs to rise."

These trends, especially as they apply in Germany, do not preclude the involvement of cooperatives – including European-wide entities such as holding cooperatives – that have been explained in this chapter. "All in all," concludes Grosskopf, "it is important to build an image of farming and horticulture that stands for small enterprises, small farms and healthy, fresh local produce that does not have to be transported over long distances."

Chapter Footnotes

1. A variation of this plan is about to be tried by Harvest States Cooperatives. It may serve as a model for others to follow, or it may reveal how the investment plan needs to be revised to serve the interests of the cooperative's members and the people Grosskopf calls "financial participants."

2. This problem has the potential of becoming greater as cooperatives perform more functions aimed at providing transaction cost services for members and customers, as cited by several experts in this book. Government services offer vivid examples, across national borders.

3. This appears to be a German phenomena in structure, but perhaps universal in practice.

4. Composition and terms on supervisory boards, as described, may be uniquely German.

5. Variations of what Grosskopf calls "the European cooperative" are emerging in the United States and Canada. And European cooperatives such as Avebe, with members in both the Netherlands and Germany, are close to fitting this description.

6. This is a German phenomena since cooperatives in most other Northern European or North American countries do not currently have shareholders who are not members. But Professor Grosskopf's point is well taken: CoBank and the St. Paul Bank for Cooperatives, in the United States; Rabobank, in the Netherlands, and other major agricultural and cooperative lenders can, in practice, become majority shareholders and force the sale of a cooperative's assets in the event of financial failure

Dr. Michael Cook

Professor Dr. Michael Cook is the Robert D. Partridge Endowed Professor in Cooperative Leadership at the University of Missouri, at Columbia, Missouri, in the central United States, where he is also director of the annual Graduate Institute of Cooperative Leadership for mid-career training of cooperative leaders, directors and managers. Born and raised on a dairy farm in Wisconsin, Professor Cook holds a B.A. degree in International Relations and History, a Master's degree in Economics and a Ph.D. degree in Agricultural Economics from the University of Wisconsin at Madison, Wisconsin.

He taught agricultural economics at the University of Wisconsin, New Mexico State University and Texas A&M University in previous academic positions. Away from his academic career, however, he has 11 years experience in executive positions with cooperatives and multinational corporations. He was president and chief executive officer of Rice Growers Association of California, a rice processing and marketing cooperative based at Sacramento, California, from 1985 through 1989; and previously served as vice president of corporate planning for Farmland Industries, America's largest farmer-owned cooperative based at Kansas City, Missouri. In that latter position, he was the president of Farmland World Trade, a trading subsidiary of the cooperative, and vice president of strategic planning for Far-Mar-Co., a Farmland joint venture marketing business.

Professor Cook was a founder of the International Food and Agribusiness Management Association, worked as a marketing manager with Tenneco Inc., served as an American Peace Corps volunteer in Montevideo, Uruguay, and was a Leadership Scholar at the United Nations. His research and lecturing activities include work in 40 countries and consulting with international organizations. Recent publications include "The Role of Management Behavior in Agricultural Cooperatives," *Journal of Agricultural Cooperatives*, 1994; "Structural Changes in the U.S. Grain and Oilseed Sector," Food and Agricultural Markets: The Quiet Revolution. National Planning Association, 1994; "The International Trade and Agricultural Policy Outlook with Implications for Farmers and Agribusinesses," abstract in *American Journal of Agricultural Economics*, 1993; with Suhler, D.R., "Origins of a Current Conflict: An Examination of Stock-Nonstock Cooperative Law," *Journal of Agricultural Cooperation*, 1993; "Strategic Management Evolution in U.S. Agricultural Cooperatives," Agricultural Cooperatives in Transition, Caski, C. and Kislev, Y., eds.; Westview Press, Boulder (Colo.) and Oxford (U.K.), 1993; and, with Barkems, A., "The Changing U.S. Pork Industry: A Dilemma for Public Policy," *Economic Review*, 1993; plus more than 50 other published chapters, research papers and essays for books, periodicals and professional journals.

A VIEW FROM NORTH AMERICA:

NEW GENERATION COOPERATIVES AS AN ALTERNATIVE APPROACH

By Lee Egerstrom

A close look at the career of Dr. Michael Cook shows a life devoted to educating and leading people through changes in "mindsets."

It is an important part of his work at the University of Missouri where he holds a special, endowed chair to teach cooperative leadership in the Department of Agricultural Economics. Graduate students come to the Missouri campus from throughout the world to study changes in cooperative structures and strategies.

It was important when he headed world trading activities at Farmland Industries, the large farmer-owned supply and marketing cooperative in the central U.S. states. Like Dutch and Danish cooperatives, Farmland concluded early on that growth had to come from business activities stretching beyond its own farm supply territories. And it was especially important later, before taking the academic post at the University of Missouri, when he served as president of the Rice Growers Association cooperative in California.

"With the Rice Growers, we had to change thinking – change our identity – from being commodity oriented to being product oriented," he says.

It represents a change of mindsets that farmers are wrestling with in many of the large, agricultural exporting and industrialized nations of the world, Professor Cook adds. "The challenge is to change when you've been comfortable with your cooperative being a user organization for farm supplies or marketing commodities."

Professor Cook's work strikes a close resemblance to the internal examinations going on inside Dutch cooperatives today, and externally throughout Europe by farmers, their cooperatives' boards and managers, academic researchers and educators, and government agricultural and marketing specialists. The structures and strategies of cooperatives, public policies and marketing arrangements are all being questioned – or should be – as local and national food systems become integrated into a new, global food system, he says.

Exploring options

"Dutch (and all) farmers have to realize they have the option to be or not be part of the global food chain," Professor Cook says. Tied up in the process of selecting which option to follow are three central issues facing cooperative businesses worldwide: Ownership issues, control issues and dilution of benefits issues. Where cooperatives haven't been able to restructure themselves to satisfy those issues, farmers have decided to merge, convert to investor-owned firms, such as stock companies, or sell their assets to other companies in the global food system.

"Agricultural producers in Holland have until recently been very comfortable with the concept of the traditional agriculture and food institutions," he says. "They were producer/user-owned and producer/user-controlled. Benefits, and payments, were in relationship of use.

"The user organizations usually had their roots in defensive actions whereby it was in the interest of members to pool the value of their assets for help with buying or marketing. Now, the Netherlands / Dutch environment has changed. This environment suggests that if producers want to capitalize, or derive benefits from their cooperatives, they will have to be more offensive minded."

This shift in mindset often causes friction among different members of cooperatives in the United States, and is likely to do so in the

Netherlands if it changes member relationships with the cooperatives, he adds. "By being a more offensive marketing system, the cooperatives will become more investor-driven than user-driven. That is a dramatic change in the mindset of the organization."

Regardless how cooperatives choose to restructure themselves, Professor Cook says the change can be evolutionary where cooperatives have already achieved product manufacturing and international marketing success. By those actions, the cooperatives have been moving towards offensive strategies.

"Investor-driven, producer-owned and controlled organizations can be sensitive to producer needs, and user-driven organizations can be sensitive to investors. But their boards will have to decide which strategy is foremost. They will decide how benefits of membership are derived," he says.

If farmers want to create a business environment in which there is a "high probability of success" for their cooperatives, he adds, they will need an offensive strategy instead of a defensive strategy. Moreover, they may need to restructure their cooperatives and actually create new investor-driven institutions.

It should be noted that neither the traditional, defensive cooperative nor the new, offensive enterprise is outside the concept of farmers seeking countervailing power, as described by Canadian-American John Kenneth Galbraith in the 1950s and 1960s. Professor Galbraith's work, which continues to be an inspiration for European cooperatives, dealt with imperfections in the marketplace. The offensive cooperative is addressing the imperfection of existing markets to return sufficient income and proportion of food industry revenues to the producers.

North American farmers, including those in Canada, are facing similar environmental changes and are also becoming aware of the need for offensive strategies, Professor Cook says. But there are different models being developed for cooperative organizations because of differences between North American and European countries. North American farmers have far less control of marketing most farm products through cooperatives. In addition to these structural differences in food systems, Cook notes there are regulatory and cultural differences as well. These differences serve as benchmarks for cooperatives considering changes in structures and strategies, and thus cooperatives will need different models to follow as they contemplate change. Regardless of the models, the objectives will be similar.

New Generation Cooperatives

Creating new cooperative organizations called "new generation cooperatives" (NGCs) is becoming popular in the United States. They start with an offensive business strategy aimed at gaining income and profits for members from cooperatively-owned processing plants and jointly-owned production units. More than 100 of these new enterprises have been formed since 1991 in the two states of Minnesota and North Dakota, and farmers' investment in starting these businesses was approaching $2 billion (U.S.) by late 1995.

In a booklet explaining these enterprises to Canadian farmers, economists at the University of Saskatchewan Centre for the Study of Co-operatives says New Generation Cooperatives have three common bonds:(1)

• "They represent the newest generation of cooperatives; earlier generations emerged in the 1920s and then again in the 1940s;

• "Their major focus is value-added processing, representing a departure from the main objective of commodity marketing held by their predecessors; and

• "Rather than acting as clearinghouses for product, a NGC is restricted to only accepting a predetermined amount of product from its members. In fact, a 'two-way' contract exists between members and the cooperative that requires the member to deliver a certain amount of product to the cooperative and requires the cooperative to take delivery of this product." (2)

Professor Cook notes that there is a key element in cooperative ownership that underlies the three items above. It is the investor-driven strategy of the new cooperatives. They are "closed" membership cooperatives, not the open, user-driven cooperatives of past, defensive farmer-owned companies. Curt Watson, a farmer from Renville, Minnesota, who has helped start four new generation cooperatives in his home community since 1991, describes it this way: "You have to pay to play. And when all members have invested in the cooperative, you have 100 percent of your membership working to make it a successful business enterprise." (3)

These new cooperatives include such business enterprises as using members' grains to feed large numbers of pigs, laying hens, beef cattle and bison (buffalo); processing farm commodities into industrial products, local cheeses not produced by the members' other dairy cooperatives, and specialty food products. At the same time, these new ventures closely follow paths taken earlier by farmers who produce a number of special crops, says Professor Cook.

Citrus farmers in Florida, Texas and California have similar cooperatives with closed memberships. Ocean Spray, a large cooperative owned by cranberry growers in Massachusetts and Wisconsin, have operated what could now be called a new generation cooperative for more than 50 years. And in the Minnesota-North Dakota region of the American Middle West, sugar beet growers have done the same by forming cooperatives to buy an existing sugar beet factory (American Crystal Sugar) and starting two new sugar cooperatives, Southern Minnesota Beet Sugar Co. and Minn-Dak Growers Association.

Those three farmer-owned cooperatives were started in the early 1970s and provide models for the recently created new generation cooperatives in the Midwest. (4)

Professor Cook is updating a taxonomy that describes cooperative structures to more clearly define new generation cooperatives, but it is a work in progress; they may change as rapidly as creative producers find new ways to gather larger revenues and profits from processing and marketing.

At the present time, Cook identifies seven structural types of agricultural-related cooperatives operating in the United States. They include the Farm Credit System (farm finance), Rural Utilities (including electricity, telephone service and, more recently, rural cable television systems), Bargaining Cooperatives, Marketing Cooperatives, Local Associations (a local, geographical cooperative that usually belongs to a large regional cooperative that has federated members), Multi-functional Regional Cooperatives (they can be federated or centralized and perform diverse services for members), and the New Generation Cooperatives. (5)

Many of these cooperative structures would compare with Dutch institutions and those developed in other European countries. Regulatory and cultural differences, as Professor Cook noted earlier, would make close comparisons difficult, however.

But broadly viewed, particularly in looking at strategies and structures, there are comparisons that can be helpful in serving as models when farmers look beyond national boundaries in search of models. "Farmers appear to learn best from other farmers. There is a high level of trust," he says, which explains the importance of searching for models that can be used as patterns during times of change.

A big question, then, is how should large cooperative businesses adopt new generation cooperative – or investor-driven – strategies when they've already achieved great success in the Netherlands, Denmark and other countries with similar agricultural histories?

Farming for the 'bottom line'

Professor Cook says farmers in Holland should address that question from the same premise as farmers in North America. "The bottom line is that (income from) your raw material is going to go down. Redevelopment in Eastern Europe. International competition. Public policies. Production constraints. Capital needs. A lot of influences will limit the price you receive and production on your land resources.

"On the other hand, you might see demand grow for limited (plantings) of specialty crops, of identity preserved crops, like new varieties of corn or special potatoes.

"Taken together, cooperatives are looking at only two options. They can diversify, or they can move vertically through the food chain. Obviously, the Dutch cooperatives are doing both."

For cooperatives to complete this process, Cook says farmers must have a change of mindset and see their cooperatives as similar to an investor-owned firm. In turn, boards of directors and managers of cooperatives must also act as operators of investor-owned firms, "always asking how diversification, an acquisition, or a new venture will help their member-investors," he says.

This process, and change of mindset, are causing cooperatives worldwide to reexamine themselves and reappraise their structures and strategies. This is being done three ways, Cook says.

First, traditional cooperatives are redefining their business approach, he says. This includes looks at needs for capitalization, user or investor ownership rights, and control. Second, they are also looking at restructuring their businesses. This usually involves investment in more value-added activities, more global activities such as investments and acquisitions in new markets. And third, cooperatives are looking at ways to be involved in production.

"One and Number Three are not always viable options," he said. In fact, he adds, constraints on finding options may be causing some cooperatives to disband, or convert to becoming investor-owned firms (IOFs) under different business ownership schemes.

Several Irish cooperatives have converted to IOF companies in recent years, he said. And Cook knows of a rice growers cooperative in the

United States that converted to private ownership in 1987. Mississippi Chemical, a petroleum and fertilizer refining and supply cooperative, recently made a similar conversion.

The third choice, or option, available to cooperatives comes with sensitive issues to be resolved with existing members. These companies must determine an appropriate role in basic production when that has been the primary function of their members.

New Generation Cooperatives, like those being created in the United States and in parts of former Communist countries, may be filling voids left by large cooperatives and national agricultural systems that didn't resolve how they could help members derive benefits from value-added processing or marketing services.(6) It is just as probable that memberships held cooperative boards and managers back from involvement in food and fiber production, even when it could be shown that vertical forms of agriculture would have helped most if not all the cooperative's members. (7)

By expanding abroad, into Asia, Africa, Eastern Europe and South America, cooperatives can become involved in production with a strategy of being more vertically involved in developing food systems. To a lesser extent, Dutch cooperatives are involved with North American cooperatives, private investors and agribusiness companies through joint venture arrangements. But there may be fewer opportunities for having a role in production; the U.S. and Canadian food and agriculture industries are as developed, and mature, as Europe's.

But linkages with New Generation Cooperatives through various legal partnerships and joint venture schemes may be helpful to traditional cooperatives, Professor Cook notes. The new entities have resolved issues to cooperative property rights and "free rider" memberships (8), have asset appreciation mechanisms, delivery right mechanisms, proportional patronage distribution, base equity capital plans and membership policies controlling entrance in the venture in by-laws and operating practices. (9)

Universal challenges for cooperatives

Graduate students from Greece, the United Kingdom, Argentina, Brazil and developing African nations have come to the University of Missouri to study cooperative business issues and leadership under Professor Cook. They come to Missouri, in part, because Cook holds the Robert Partridge chair that has been endowed by American cooperatives and is devoted to the study of cooperative leadership. They also come because the issues facing cooperatives are universal; the choices and need for change are different only because cooperative laws and regulations differ from one country to the next, and because different countries have cultural anomalies that will shape, limit or expand options for change.

The university sits in a small college town of Columbia, midway between Missouri's two large cities. St. Louis, on the banks of the Mississippi River on the east edge of the state, is a major industrial center and a shipping center along America's most important intercoastal waterway system. Kansas City, along the Missouri River on the state's western border with Kansas, is a major agribusiness and agricultural marketing center. Columbia is clearly a geopolitical compromise location for the state's large public university. MFA Inc. and MFA Oil Co., two farm supply cooperatives of common heritage, share the academic community with the university. But there is little industry located there.

For Professor Cook, his faculty colleagues and students, however, Columbia, Missouri, does offer a vantage point to watch developments with cooperative businesses throughout the world and in the major agricultural states and provinces of North America. In October, 1995, cooperative business publications had news stories about the restructuring and redefining of the Rice Growers Association of California. A transformation, started in the 1980s when Cook was its chief executive officer, is now complete. Instead of trying to sell all rice produced by its members, the cooperative now takes proportionate quantities of top-quality rice for which it can provide marketing services. Members sell their surplus or inferior grade rice to the existing commodity market. This doesn't dilute the members' economic benefits; it increases the cooperative's payments to members and the members' return on investments.

In a strategic sense, the rice growers' organization has become similar to a New Generation Cooperative and predecessors of the new ventures, such as Ocean Spray and California's own Blue Diamond edible nuts cooperative.

It is a transformation that is being duplicated by successful cooperatives throughout the world, it should be noted.

"This was accomplished after I left," Cook says of the rice growers' strategic changes. "What they've accomplished is turning from being commodity oriented to being product oriented.."

Chapter Footnotes

1. Stefanson, Brenda; Fulton, Murray and Harris, Andrea. *New Generation Cooperatives: Rebuilding Rural Economies*. Centre for the Study of Co-operatives, University of Saskatchewan . 1995.

2. Ibid.

3. From "*Reviving Renville: A Cooperative Approach to Development*," A film produced by the Minnesota Association of Cooperatives, St. Paul, Minnesota.

4. Egerstrom, Lee. Make No Small Plans: A Cooperative Revival for Rural America. Lone Oak Press. 1995.

5. Cook, Michael. *Food and Agricultural Marketing Issues for the 21st Century*. The Food and Agriculture Marketing Consortium, University of Missouri, 1993, reprinted in Egerstrom, Make No Small Plans.

6. This is the writer's observation, not from Professor Cook. See the following footnote.

7. A case for this scenario is offered in Egerstrom, Make No Small Plans. Co-op Country Farmers Elevator, at Renville, Minnesota, explored entry in the pig industry to raise the value of the elevator co-op members' grains by preparing it as value-added pig feed. The cooperative's members voted against the plan after some farmers worried it would make their company a competitor with their own farm. A group of the cooperative's members used the plan, however, and formed ValAdCo cooperative at Renville in 1991. ValAdCo now has 38 farm family members, has 52 employees at four confinement barn sites, and its members jointly own 10,000 sows. In late 1995, ValAdCo was exploring a pork slaughtering venture that would likely be a joint venture cooperative with either Danish or Dutch cooperatives. If it builds pig slaughtering and pork processing facilities, it would also provide a nearby market for other Coop Country Farmers Elevator members who are now raising pigs or may choose to in the future.

8. Van Dijk, Gert. "*Kaapital in de dode hand.*" A paper published by Nationale Cooperatieve Raad, The Hague, the Netherlands, which examines "free rider" issues for cooperatives.

9. Cook. In Make No Small Plans. Restated during interview for this book, 1995.

Part Four: Defining Local Farm and Community Interests in New, Global Markets

PROFESSOR ARIE VAN DER ZWAN

Professor Dr. Arie van der Zwan, born 1935, studied economics at the Netherlands Higher College of Economics (now Erasmus University), Rotterdam, graduating in 1960. His Ph.D. degree was obtained at the University of Amsterdam in 1968. He became a market researcher and advisor after completing his national service.

He was appointed associate professor of Commerce and Market Research at Erasmus in 1972, and was appointed a member of the Advisory Council on Government Policy in 1978. He chaired the Council's working group that prepared the report, "The Role and Future of Dutch Industry," in 1980. This report played an important role in the re-evaluation of business and industry in the 1980s.

Dr. van der Zwan also served on the Wagener Commissions that were created in 1981 and 1982 to advise the government on industrial policy. In 1983, he was appointed president-director of the National Investment Bank (NIB), leading it through the transformation into a private investment bank and later taking it public on the Amsterdam Stock Exchange.

He left the bank in 1988 to join Vendex International and, in 1989, he took a third appointment as president-director of World Software Group BV. Concurrent with those positions in the business world, Dr. van der Zwan was installed as professor of the endowed chair of Commercial Policy and Management at Erasmus. In 1994, he was appointed professor of the endowed chair on the study of the Development of the Welfare State at Utrecht University. In addition, Van der Zwan has been working as an independent consultant on policy and management since 1992.

He is the author of a great many publications on marketing policy and research, economics, and policy and management.

A LOOK AT GLOBAL AND LOCAL SOCIETY:

NEW COOPERATIVES AND COTTAGE INDUSTRIES AS WEAPONS OF OPPORTUNITIES FOR PRODUCERS, WORKERS, COMMUNITIES
By Dr. Gert van Dijk and Pieter Bos

All throughout Europe, and indeed, the entire industrialized world, people are wrestling with questions about their economic future, where they may find future employment, and economic opportunities to sustain and secure their livelihoods.

"Unbridled internationalism" has thrown labor markets into disarray and led to social dislocation, says Professor Arie van der Zwan. In time, he suspects, this social upheaval will lead to governmental and social reactions.

"People aren't prepared to have their lot determined by large corporations that see the market (only) as a sales outlet, then move on with their revenues to invest elsewhere," he says. A countervailing check on these trends, he says, may be the revival of the cooperative philosophy – not only within agriculture but other sectors of the economy as well.

Cottage industry cooperatives

"I expect a new style of cooperative to evolve, based on (a type of) barter trading: If you're prepared to buy my products, then I'm prepared to buy yours, or to cover your firm's risks," he says.

Operating on a smaller scale will become an important part in this development, in Van der Zwan's opinion. "High technology will make it possible to return to highly developed cottage and craft industries. The value added within the firm is the source of extra income and employment."

But this won't evolve on its own, the expert on industrial policy warns. Experiments in operating on a small scale will be necessary, he says, and these ventures will have to propagate the philosophy by example.(1)

Van der Zwan believes large, established cooperatives will have only a minor role in this industrial transformation process. They may, however, be confronted with the results of these changes, in the form of growing competition in sales markets or strategic alliances with the local cooperatives.**(2)**

"At high school and during my studies at university, a reasonable amount of attention was paid to cooperatives," he recalls. "Unfortunately, I must agree that today there is little interest in the (cooperative) 'phenomenon'. This is not only the case for the cooperative but for all non-commercial institutions in the economy.**(3)** Their importance, is, in my opinion, grossly underestimated," he says.

There are two causes of this current neglect by academic institutions, he says.

First, there is a belief in the analytical approach that is not prepared to accept an independent role for institutions; and second, he adds, is the influence of the economic school of thought that "has declared the market mechanism sacred and labels anything that hinders that mechanism as an aberration, or deviant. Interest in institutions in the economy has dwindled as a result of these two forces."

But there are reasons for hope, he continues. Citing a recent inaugural lecture of Professor F. van Waarden at Utrecht University, in which he expounded on the theme of institutions, Van der Zwan said interest in institutions is being revived.

Life cycles

Professor van der Zwan doesn't restrict his comments to just agricultural cooperatives. "We used to have consumer cooperatives," he says, recalling Dutch experiences. "At the turn of the last century, they were very powerful and were able to maintain their influence for quite some time, (at least) up until the end of World War II. It was only afterwards when their influence began to ebb." And beyond them, he adds, the Dutch have had building contractor cooperatives, and housing cooperatives based on cooperative principles still exist.

An interesting question then arises, he says, as to why cooperatives were so much stronger, more expansive, and more innovative during the first half of this century than during the latter half. No doubt, he explains, that they have been influenced by the cyclical nature that affects all firms and organizations: birth, growth, flourish, stagnation and decline.

"At a certain moment even cooperatives lose the vigor and enthusiasm with which they began," he says. "Often they no longer fulfill the need amongst their members that originally led to their creation.

Once this happens they become, in fact, businesses that must compete with the large investor-owned firms. They are usually at a disadvantage in the ensuing struggle because they still carry the cooperative baggage they acquired during the earlier phases of their life cycle. Unfortunately, this baggage no longer contributes to their performance and is thus a burden."

Life cycles of agricultural cooperatives can also be characterized by some of these phases, observes Van der Zwan. "Sometimes I wonder whether the risks borne by farmer-members of some of the now extremely large production-oriented cooperatives have not become too great. In such instances, perhaps, farmer-members would do better to transform their production-oriented cooperative into a market-oriented cooperative (suppliers' cooperative)." This would free the resulting large processing firm to operate as any competitive investor-owned firm without the cooperative ballast, he says. And, he adds, this would allow the firm to determine its own purchasing policy for raw materials and to choose an optimal financial structure for its operations.

New Flourish

A new sort of firm is needed to guarantee the continuity of firms as vehicles of enterprise, he says. "Not only the life of man is limited; enterprises do not enjoy eternal life, either. At a certain moment, a 'new' person is necessary to ensure the continuity of mankind," he says in offering an analogy.

This doesn't mean the old firm is doomed. Van der Zwan says many such companies will choose a different course of action that will make them flourish once again.

He offers several examples:

"The old shipping lines at the turn of the last century were flourishing businesses at the top of the commercial pyramid," he recalls. "They are now investment companies – something completely different."

The Holland-America Line is one specific example, he says. And the old railroad companies in the United States followed a similar route, to a great extent.

After the Second World War, steel companies were the envy of all, he adds. "Bethlehem Steel was then a firm in its prime." And six years ago, he notes, IBM shares were at the top of the Blue Chip pile. "What is left of these last two today?" (4) These two companies had inadequate responses to changes in the market.

There are times when companies can take advantages of changes in markets; at other times, they are at a loss to deal with change, he says. "It is then that new forms of enterprise are necessary to discover the adaptations needed to master the market again." (5)

The transformation from a production-oriented cooperative to a market-oriented cooperative is not an inevitable progression, he further explains. It will bring benefits to its members in many instances. But in other cases, he says, "one could expect that continuing on the same course will bring the most benefit, even though some difficulties must be overcome."

Property titles

Discussions throughout the Western industrialized nations about regulating the financial interests of cooperative members have astounded Van der Zwan. Accounting firms, among other business organizations, already offer helpful models for handling and transferring property titles.

A solution to the problem of hand these financial interests is "a simple matter" of making cooperative members' property titles similar in character to real property titles. "You can make them transferable by, for example, registering them on the unlisted exchange of the stocks and bonds market. (6)

"Often, the unlisted exchange is used in share trading to establish the value of a particular share. Moreover, you can exert some influence on the unlisted exchange," he explains. For example, a cooperative might start a financial institution to offer new members the opportunity to buy shares in their cooperative. The institution would finance the purchase by using the shares as collateral. "It is really quite simple."

Creating the financial organization for this purpose should be simple for cooperative lending banks such as Holland's Rabobank. And it would be easy to maintain usual rules and regulations for share trading under such a system, he says. "Members cannot sell their share to anyone. They would be compelled to offer them to other members or, alternatively, the cooperative could arrange for them to be made available to new members as they join. That sort of thing is common in accounting partnerships," he says.

Accountants leaving a partnership receive "compensation," which is paid for by new accountants joining the partnership. The new members, or partners, do not have to pay immediately, he says; rather, they pay over time through adjustments in their income. "In short, there are so many ways of overcoming any of the drawback of property titles that I am always surprised that the problem still occurs in practice."

Renewal of the cooperative philosophy

It is unclear how existing cooperatives will develop and fare in the future. However, Professor van der Zwan is convinced that it's just a matter of time before there is a renewal of the cooperative philosophy. For him, one of the most critical problems facing modern society – and not just agriculture – is the task of creating work and securing a livelihood.

A revival of the cooperative philosophy would go part of the way toward solving this problem, in his opinion. But he does not expect existing cooperatives to bear the burden of this renewal.

"We are going to return to a barter system, and cooperatives will be organized around the principles of bartering," he says in offering an opinion on future developments. "If you're prepared to buy my products, then I'm prepared to buy yours, or to cover your firm's risks in some way. (7)

"You see, what we've lost is control of our markets," he explains. "Within our national borders, we used to have a balance of sales and production. Our system of trading was based on exchange, in a quite literal sense of the word. What was imported was paid for by what was exported. As a consequence, demand for labor and its supply were in equilibrium.

"Unfortunately, that balance is at the point of becoming completely disrupted by all these multinational firms that operate in our markets but are no longer prepared or able to offer the employment that is intrinsically concomitant to the purchase of their products. Our destiny is now tied to these large corporations, which see in our markets a sales opportunity but not a place to invest their takings. They reinvest them in more attractive markets in other countries of their choice," he says. (8)

Van der Zwan, in what is probably a departure from most current economics and trade literature, says he's convinced that national governments will regain some control of their markets to reinstate a healthy balance between buying and selling. "Perhaps that sounds a bit old-fashioned," he says. "I know many colleagues and schools of thought preach that only global economics has a satisfactory future to offer. I don't believe them!"

He blames "unbridled internationalization" for disrupting the balance, and says it must be brought under control because the social dislocation it causes is too great. He adds that international business will not welcome any such control, which will lead to a trend where consumers join the debate through the use of their purchasing power.

Cooperatives are ideally situated to effect a balance, he says. If they can continue to combine enough purchasing power, they can develop selling power. "Thus, we have returned to the time-honored cooperative principle in which cooperation is the basis of our livelihood," he says.

A good example of shared interests – the basis of a barter system – was seen at the turn of the last century, Van der Zwan explains. At that time, Dutch buyers' (consumers) cooperatives also became produce (sellers') cooperatives. Consumers could find quality produce at reasonable prices in their neighborhood stores. And on the other hand, he says, employment was ensured because the cooperative bought the same produce from factories they had founded for that purpose. "This is a clear example, I think, of a principle we are likely to hear more about," he says.

Rediscovering and mastering this principle won't necessarily come easy. But, says Van der Zwan, "Just start experimenting with it. That should lead to new, successful initiatives. To date, there has been too little experimentation in business," he adds, claiming far too few new forms of business have been created or attempted.

Van der Zwan says he can describe an interesting theory for a business based on principles, but it isn't enough to believe it will work. "It must be implemented; the proof of the pudding is in the eating," he says. "These things need modification and refinement and that begins with small-scale experiments."

Common interests

"You should recognize," instructs Van der Zwan, "that innovation is stimulated by trend setters and pioneers, be it in the industrial or agricultural sector." Others will follow the trend setters and pioneers when success is observed, he adds. Opportunists follow in their wake, recognizing the chances and taking the risks. "So you see, one is fired by ideals, the other by profits. If all goes well, a critical mass is reached after which continuity is guaranteed."

As an example, Van der Zwan points to a research project he worked on that explored the possibility of a cooperative venture for growing cannabis. "Perhaps not such a fortunate example, but it does illustrate my approach clearly," he says. (9) A few farmers and Van der Zwan looked at trying to develop a way to cultivate cannabis as a commercial crop. If a firm interested in processing the cannabis didn't have the capital it needed for the project, it could make a proposal to the farmers, he adds. The farmers could receive a contract for selling the cannabis to the firm if they invested in the firm. It wouldn't matter if the firm was a cooperative, he says. "No one is going to stop you from basing your contractual relations on cooperative principles."

That is the main point Van der Zwan says he wants to make. Cooperative principles can be the foundation upon which all contractual relations are laid, he says. "If common interests no longer exist, where the element of barter is absent, then the cooperative is no longer viable"

If that is so, he continues, farmers should look for new opportunities, new crops, for processing agricultural raw materials. Only by encouraging this sort of experimentation on a wide scale can breakthroughs be expected. "That won't be easy," he admits, "because farmers, like other workers, have not learned to take initiatives in matters concerning their own livelihood. Farmers, and the rest of the work force, will have to learn once more to use their ingenuity and not wait for their problems to be solved for them." It is through experimentation and setting up new forms of cooperatives, Van der Zwan says, that will allow farmers to "come to grips" with their business and economic problems.

Barter agents

Van der Zwan is not shouting, "Stop the world! I want to get off!" Instead, he says, there is more to his idea than he's been describing.

"If you want this barter trade to flourish, then you are going to need some sort of barter agent who will be able to operate on an international level and also bring the smaller cooperatives in contact with each other," he says. A cooperative should be able to request a trading partner to these agents and leave it to them to find one. "We used to trade with countries behind the Iron Curtain this way," he notes. "You have a product, you put it on offer, an intermediary registers your request and looks for a trading partner for you: 'find me a partner who is prepared to take delivery of my product and I will be prepared to accept another product of his in return.' It would be unrealistic for you to make all the arrangements yourself – the transaction costs are too high," he says. (10)

Such arrangements are best left to specialists, says Van der Zwan, who adds there is a useful role for such professionals. "It would be great if a new cooperative movement was to grow that had as one of its aims the development of this sort of intermediary role. Such a 'superstructure' would be a prerequisite for the success of smaller cooperatives," he explains.(11)

Van der Zwan expects that less raw materials will be processed in corporately-owned factories in the future, and that more will be processed on a smaller scale, probably in locally-owned factories. Raw produce, or commodities, should pass through the marketing-distribution chain by barter trading, he insists. "But, if you really want to develop this principle, then you will have to promote it in communities, villages and regions, so that it takes root in people's minds," he says.

"I expect employment opportunities to become such a scarce commodity in the next few decades that it will permeate and influence people's outlooks so much that they will be prepared to restructure their communities on principles different from those applied today," Van der Zwan explains. "Up until now, the principle has been, 'I work in a job for money and I buy where I can get the best deal, even if I have to drive 25 kilometers to do so.' I think the new principle will be something like, 'I buy where I can support employment, on the understanding that those I buy from will help me to remain employed'."

Processing your own raw produce

Van der Zwan is convinced farmers must process their raw produce themselves. "They have the tide with them. Who, these days, wants to eat food that has come out of a factory?" (12)

Moreover, he says, farmers have no choice. "Look," he says, "farmers have specialized, too, and in no small measure. The agricultural sector has seen tremendous gains in productivity as a result. But the enormous surpluses that are also partly due to this now threaten disaster. Perhaps there has been too much specialization."

The economist suggests backwards integration is needed – or in the case of farmers, forward integration. "Look at it this way, if I'm running a farm that also processes its own raw produce, there is less need and opportunity for me to farm larger areas. (13) An increase in added value can be realized through intensification, particularly when extensive farming has got out of hand."

Dutch agriculture has promoted increased specialization and differentiation to ensure that its produce is amongst the cheapest in the world, Van der Zwan says. But, he believes, this competition has become untenable.

"Circumstances here (the Netherlands) are no longer favorable for this," he says. "For every crop we grow, there is somewhere else in the world where conditions, e.g. climate, are more favorable." Besides, he says, the land resources are too limited for Dutch farmers. "That's why I think it would be a blessing if specialization was to be reversed so that value could be added through refining your own raw produce."

Van der Zwan said he's convinced Dutch agriculture is headed for disaster if farmers continue to compete by increasing productivity, especially now that trade is less regulated. It is tragic, he says, that farmers work so hard for so little profit while their survival is always threatened. It is for those reasons that he thinks farmers have to accept new forms of organization that will support them in their struggle for survival. And even with the presence of cooperatives in most agricultural sectors in the Netherlands, he says, farmers are still trying to do too much on their own. "An example can be seen close to where I live, in Tholen," he says. "Farmers grow asparagus there. It is lucrative, but it is also very hard work. Even then, you have to sell your produce at the farm gate to passers-by. In my opinion, this represents an unbearable risk. Perhaps these farmers would be better off forming a marketing cooperative together or employing a sales representative."

Return to cottage industries

In Van der Zwan's view, the future of agriculture lies in refining, or processing, your own raw produce. No only do farmers have little choice, he says, but they would be missing a tide of opportunity – both from a marketing and a technological perspective.

"A return, to some extent, to cottage industry is part of my vision," he says. "It is remarkable that we have neglected and rejected cottage industry here (the Netherlands), yet it Italy it is still well developed." Restarting cottage industry will require more ingenuity, creativity and problem-solving skills than money, he adds.

"This won't happen overnight. Decades are needed. Nevertheless, you must begin somewhere or it will never take off."

Van der Zwan doesn't expect much assistance from large corporations in bringing this about. "Their point of focus is the big picture. Why? Simply because from their perspective only large-scale operations make sense; small-scale operations don't fit their cost structure.(14) The sorts of experiments I'm talking about would never make it in their hands; they are all too small scale to do so. That's why we have to emphasize another scale of enterprise, and why I call it – not entirely by accident – cottage industry..."

Cottage industry has an image more closely associated with quality than has large-scale industry, he adds. "That is why I don't think it is out of step with current market trends – rather the opposite!"

Brand names are losing their power

One reason why cottage industries have greater opportunities ahead results from brand names losing their control of the market, Van der Zwan says. Exclusiveness is becoming a greater force in the market, and consumers associate exclusiveness with superior quality, exquisite aromas and an exclusive image.

"The 'magic' of brand names is diminishing all over the world," he notes. In Holland, for instance, he cites that Douwe Egberts – a roaster of popular coffees and maker of various consumer food products – is losing market share ground to the growing number of retail chain brands. And retail chains are also becoming more interested in craft products. Exclusive products become attractive to retail chains that are trying to find ways to distinguish themselves from their competition. "A supermarket chain such as Albert Heijm (Holland's largest supermarket chain) is quite capable of decentralizing its buying for this," he says.

The second factor he sees that makes cottage industry and crafts attractive and viable is the revolution occurring in the means of production. "With modern technology, it is possible to make high-quality products on a small scale for a low unit cost and at optimum levels of quality control and management," he says. Take roasting coffee, for example. These days, you can do it in a shop, and there are many shops doing it. As you step through the shop door, the rich aroma of roasting coffee beans surrounds you."

Back to small-scale enterprise

"Yes," continues Van der Zwan, "that is the paradox of our time. With today's technology, we can return to cottage industries where levels of sophistication are high. Besides, the products offered are much more attractive than those coming from a (large) factory. I think this potential is not utilized as much as it could be. Before, increases in scale of operation were introduced into agriculture because this was a prerequisite for optimizing benefits to be gained there. Unfortunately, the sector has not yet recognized the benefits that could follow on from a reduction in scale."

The highest degree of industriousness today can be seen in activities that are, in fact, highly developed cottage industries, insists Van der Zwan. "Printing is a good example of this! Thanks to computers, even small print shops are quite capable of printing periodicals (magazines, etc.). That is remarkable! Modern computers have made it possible to design print materials in ways that would have been unthinkable before." (15)

Van der Zwan sees a dual system of production and manufacturing developing while production returns to basics. For agriculture and all sorts of crafts, he says, ingenious machines will be invented that make it possible for small firms to compete successfully with large firms. Not in every respect, he admits, but certainly as far as exclusiveness and craftsmanship are concerned. Disadvantages can be compensated for by participating in organizational structures, such as the barter trading agencies he's described.

Nevertheless, Van der Zwan warns that it is "unrealistic to expect the world to return to a small-scale (production) existence. I expect the world to become more pluralistic. You can already see this in the fashion industry. Variety in designs is on the increase. Alongside large-volume articles you can also find small-volume, exclusive articles," he says.

Such dualism is also likely in the agricultural sector, says Van der Zwan, although the main-stream offerings will be produced in bulk. Put another way, there will be room in the world food industry for small-scale or smaller-scaled "product" production even though agriculture will be dominated by commodity production.

He warns there will be friction between the large-scale firms and cottage industries started by producers. "Our society may, in theory, champion pluralism; but in practice, uniformity too often wins the day," he says. This uniformity is compatible with large-scale production, he says, while for agriculture "the fruits of the harvest have become bitter to the tongue.

"The time has come to harvest other fruits!"

Chapter Footnotes

1. The Basque people in the Mondragon region of Northern Spain have already provided models of successful industrial/worker cooperatives, although their manufacturing successes with household

appliances and automobile component parts have progressed far beyond the definition of cottage industries.

2. See chapter on Professor Grosskopf and formation of cooperative holding companies.

3. The terminology of "non-commercial institutions" may be misleading to readers in various countries. In the United States, for instance, cooperatives must be profit-making commercial and service enterprises to retain their legal status as a cooperative. Moreover, they would be considered an "organization," not an "institution;" but in this case Van der Zwan is combining the two to separate them from the traditional privately-held and publicly-traded stock companies.

4. Both Bethlehem Steel and IBM are having a rebound, it should be noted, after taking remedial actions to bounce back from the times referred to by Professor van der Zwan.

5. Van der Zwan's point is well taken in regards to the U.S. steel industry. The rapid development of what are called "mini-mills," which use smaller, electric arc furnaces instead of the traditional, coal-fired blast furnace technology, has revived the U.S. steel industry in the mid-1990s.

6. A form of this is offered by sugar beet, corn, vegetable and other value-added, or New Generation Cooperatives, found in the United States.

7. This comment, and following observations, become a clear description of ways cooperatives can reduce or eliminate transaction costs for their members and trading partners.

8. North American readers might see a parallel with earnings made in Iowa, or Manitoba, being removed to Los Angeles and New York or Toronto and Montreal. And that was before the earnings were likely to be moved and invested abroad.

9. Perhaps not. People have trouble taking the cannabis plant seriously because of its popular abuse. But it was an important crop raised by Midwestern U.S. farmers during World War II and was used as a substitute for a large number of fiber products, including the making of ropes for the U.S. Navy.

10. It should be noted that some large cooperatives have barter trade units in place that essentially attempt to work such trades. It should also be noted that some economists – especially in the United States – criticize barter trade for eliminating "multiplier effects" that create new wealth even though it may be a convenient disposal mechanism for surplus production.

11. See Nilsson, discussion of European holding company cooperatives.

12. Semantics and culture come into play with Van der Zwan's reference to a "factory," and it may not be understood in North America. It can be equated to discussions of "factory farming" in North America, and extended to discussions of who owns the factory where food products are processed and manufactured. But it is not necessarily at odds with Hughes and his observation that consumers want further-processed, convenient foods; see Hughes, discussion of consumer-driven food demands. Nor does it imply that farmer-supplied food products have been prepared in anything less than a state-of-the-art abattoir or processing "factory."

13. See Egerstrom, discussion of the damage of horizontal expansion of agriculture to rural communities.

14. This does not preclude the strategic alliance, or partnership arrangements, that can make a cottage industry a supplier to a large multinational. See Hughes, Nilsson, Standskov, Ruttan and Cook.

15. See North, discussion of the way technology is reducing or eliminating transaction costs.

Professor Gert van Dijk

Professor Gert van Dijk was born in Achterberg, the Netherlands, in 1946. He studied Animal Husbandry and Agricultural Economics at Wageningen Agricultural University (WAU), and Agricultural Economics at the University of Aberdeen, Scotland. He received his Ph.D. from the latter university in 1978; his thesis earned him the Albert Heijn Prize for research on the production and distribution of foodstuffs. He was Associate Professor in the Department of Agricultural Economics and Policy at WAU until 1982 when he was named head of the Agricultural Section of the National Agricultural Research Council. He was responsible in that capacity for programs dealing with social and economic research in agriculture.

Dr. van Dijk returned to WAU in 1986 where he led the Working Party for Agricultural Policy until 1990. During this period he was the secretary of the Van der Stee Committee and he wrote the report, "Beautiful Business," which exerted strong influence on agricultural policy and strategies in the Netherlands. In 1990, he was also appointed director-general of the National Council for Cooperatives in Agriculture. In that year he was also appointed Professor for the chair of Cooperative Theory at WAU, which he fills in a part-time capacity. He is also Visiting Professor at the Mediterranean Agronomy Institute in Chania, Greece. He has been an advisor to a variety of international organizations, including OECD, EAAP, the EC, PHARE, TACIS and the World Bank.

Epilogue:

The Changing Theoretical Perspective of Cooperatives and Markets

The Swiss historian Jacob Burckhardt once said that significant people are necessary to highlight an era. Because such figures carry in them both the general and the specific values of their time, the developments in that era are concentrated within them. They personify the civilization of that period, including its crises and "new deals."

These sentiments lie at the heart of this book. Its pages present people who have a good understanding of economics, politics, entrepreneurship, organization and management; people who are well versed in the theories and literature of their discipline. For this reason they have been asked to review the present state of cooperative firms in agriculture and the food industry. What is the current relationship between farmers and their cooperatives? What are the prospects for cooperatives in the agri-food sector?

Theoretical point of view

Professor Douglas North has shown clearly how neoclassical economic theories have gotten us off on the wrong foot. According to these theories, only the most technically efficient firms will survive the competition raging among them. However, this theory neglects to observe that change and harmony are never reached without friction. As the simple rhyme goes: "If everyone was wise, and did hereby well, the world would be Paradise ..." This is far from the case, and so the rhyme goes on: "... instead of often Hell."

North's message is that friction is just as important in economics as it is in physics. Unfortunately, often – if not always – misunderstanding, conflict, delay, confusion and a breakdown in business relationships are the order of the day. In modern economics such friction, a form of energy loss, is embodied in the term "transaction costs." According to the transaction cost theory, it is the most efficiently run organization – internally and externally – that will survive the competitive struggle. It is striking that everyone featured in this book agrees with this point of view.

How does this work in agricultural cooperatives?

For the cooperative as a firm, there is nothing special about this. The cooperative form of organization has to deal with the same sorts of problems and issues as all other firms; for example, dividing responsibilities between divisions and central management, or between task-oriented and process-oriented departments. However, from the point of view of a cooperative as a form of cooperation, there are some quite cooperative-specific transactions that can be identified: the fact that it cannot be taken for granted that all farmer-members have equal access to information and to technology; that cooperative firms cannot count on automatically getting approval from their members to react to new developments in consumer demand; that the cooperative firm and the farmer-members may not share the same points of view, both in the short- and the long- term; that in inward-looking cooperatives, farmers' representatives on the board may not share the same points of view as supervisors appointed from outside the cooperative, and that the involvement of members in the affairs of the cooperative can no longer be taken for granted.

Such friction should not be cause for pessimism, however. Professor Jerker Nilsson is of the opinion that such a situation also brings with it opportunities, for it is particularly within cooperative firms that the greatest experience can be found in keeping down transaction costs between primary producers and the firm.

A second conclusion could be that the strategy a cooperative is to follow, and the form given to the business relationship between the firm and the farmer's society are not matters that can be laid down for eternity. Neoclassical economic theory assumes implicitly that this is indeed the case. It views man as *Homo economicus*: always maximizing profit. That is conveniently simple and predictable. However, members are not always economically rational. Although they are in principle rational, and weigh their decisions, in practice this is not always the case. In their dealings they are all too often opportunistic, a reason for the proponents of the transaction cost theory to say: "see mankind as it is; read, for example, Machiavelli." Spontaneously the words of Alfred Marshall, founder of the neoclassical theory, come to mind, when he called the cooperative a combination of "business" and "organized trust."

Although the transaction cost theory can improve our understanding of the governance structures of organizations, I do not expect this to create any practical advantages for the boards of directors of these organizations or their managers. For the time being, Professor North's message, that in the absence of rules a process of elimination is the only approach left to follow, remains valid. Through the process of determining which sort of reorganization is out of the question, one can approach the ideal solution. In practice this means that everyone must find a creative solution for reducing their transaction costs, to prevent friction and to resolve any conflict of interests.

Management issues on the agenda

A. GLOBAL MARKETS FOR RAW AND CONSUMER PRODUCTS

Throughout this book, it has been pointed out that cooperatives will have to operate within a "global food system" in the future. Professor David Hughes describes such a system in his article as one in which the consumer rules. With this in mind, we are often encouraged to "listen to the consumer" as if they are able to specify beforehand the products they desire. Nothing could be further from the truth. "Listening" implies, in fact, creativity on the part of the firm, not only through market research and cooperation with others to develop new product-market mixes, but also by taking risks in research and market development.

Offer consumers new choices, that is the creed. If consumers choose your products you will be richly rewarded.

Everyone in this book warns farmers not to become completely dependent on the market prices, global or otherwise, of their raw produce. Forward integration (and sometimes backward integration, as in the example of genetic breeding stocks) is the strategic response. Professor Jesper Strandskov is quite clear about this: "The closer you are to the consumer, the higher your contribution can be to the proportion of the product's added value." Whatever the case, the idea that a farmer's interests stop once the wholesaler or exporter has taken delivery of their produce – without any stake in the process up until sale to the consumer – is completely behind the times.

B. PROFESSIONALISM AND SUPERVISION BY MEMBERS

The fact that farmers' interests extend beyond the farm gate has its consequences. Moving closer to the consumer means that entrepreneurs and managers will move further and further beyond the "scope" of the members of cooperatives. How, then, can members maintain their supervisory role?

It is this question that is causing Professor Werner Grosskopf's concern for German cooperatives. If management is given a completely free hand, it may undermine the very foundations of the cooperative, he fears. He recommends that board members of cooperatives call in external advisors to assist them in their duties – a practice already widespread in the Netherlands.

Strandskov, however, notes that such measures will not be enough to solve the problems Danish cooperatives are facing. He is concerned that the dominance of farmer-members on cooperative boards is in itself a limiting factor for the cooperative firm. In particular, the resolution of long-term interests is a thorny issue to tackle. For member-suppliers there is no short-term advantage in internationalization: they cannot increase production and there is no increase in income to balance any improvements in quality demanded. Their direct interests will only become apparent later, when they are operating in highly competitive markets with commensurate risks for the firm.

It is against this background that the issue of member influence becomes clear. It is not at all feasible to give hundreds of members complete access to information when decisions are being made about matters of great commercial consequence. Nevertheless, access to information and candidness are essential to maintaining unity and trust within cooperatives. Forthrightness and communication remain the essence of cooperation, as Nilsson rightly points out.

C. INVESTMENT AND RISK

The European and North American economists in this book are clear in their view that farmer-members of large cooperative firms will have to accept risks if they are to become leaders in consumer markets. There is no other way out left for them. There is an unmistakable shift towards global markets, both for agricultural raw produce and consumer products. Whoever wants to create and maintain influence in those markets must invest and accept risk. This will require members to invest in their cooperative, which should be seen as a source of income rather than a cost.

At the same time, Strandskov wonders whether Danish farmers are even able to invest, in view of their financial problems. Grosskopf, in turn, doubts German farmers are willing to invest, in which case others will have to be found to make the investments necessary in cooperative firms. If so, they will naturally expect a reward for the risks they have taken. This will, in turn, reduce the prices farmers are paid for their produce by the cooperative.

D. MEMBERS' INFLUENCE UNDER ANOTHER ORGANIZATIONAL STRUCTURE

Grosskopf's reservations are based on his expectation that members will cling to their democratic rights, as laid down in the cooperative structure, and his limited trust in their willingness to invest. I do not think this concern about developments in Germany is applicable, for example, in Denmark, the Netherlands or possibly the United States. One can, after all, take a more pragmatic approach. If members do not want to take on the role of investor, Hughes considers it quite acceptable to convert the cooperative to a partnership with the farmers possibly holding the majority of shares. In Strandskov's opinion, the pro's and con's of investment cannot be presented simply in black and white terms: risk will remain a factor in determining prices, as will the risk-bearing capital of the cooperative's members.

Professor Aire van der Zwan paints a completely different picture: one of a virtual flight of members of the large produce cooperatives back to the farm. There, they can rejuvenate the cooperative philosophy before entering the fray once again – this time in small-scale cooperatives that share common interests and, as a result, are strongly committed. In Van der Zwan's scenario, new technology will make such a reduction of scale possible. His scenario is also compatible with the cultural reactions that are expected to follow the current trend of internationalization: a renewed focus on local and regional interests.

E. INSTITUTIONAL INNOVATION AND RE-ENGINEERING

Van der Zwan's prediction approximates the New Generation Cooperatives discussed by Lee Egerstrom and Professor Michael Cook. Van der Zwan is of the opinion that the modern, large cooperative is too isolated from its members for them to be willing to invest through it. The result is that the large cooperative is now forced to watch from the sidelines as innovation, diversification and offensive strategies are developed.

This line of argument leads to the striking idea that renewal is a phenomenon unknown to the cooperative. This point of view has already been turned down as one of the shortcomings of neoclassical economic theory. Of course, organizations are improving their governance structures all the time, just as new sorts of organizations are continually being created. In this context, the induced innovation theory of Professor

Vernon Ruttan is important. This theory explains innovation within organizations in relation to external factors. What takes place within a cooperative is a reaction to stimuli from outside it.

F. FACING FACTS

One example of external factors can be seen in the Netherlands where 40 to 60 percent of the production by members must be exported. There is, moreover, little value added to much of the produce, i.e. it is exported in bulk form. This means that cooperatives will have to innovate, simply because they cannot be allowed to go under.

Even if they were so inclined, members cannot turn production on and off like a tap. Van der Zwan does not mention this point. Withdrawal from agriculture, or reducing capacity by three to four percent per year, would probably result in the collapse of rural property markets and cause a sharp fall in the value of equipment and goods that have no value outside agriculture. The financial basis of agriculture would be placed in great jeopardy. The transition from large- to small-scale agriculture is not so simple. In this light, large cooperatives will continue to be necessary, if only because they provide access to international buyers, growing ever larger, looking for opportunities to buy in bulk and so optimize the price-added value equation.

G. RETHINKING COOPERATIVE GOALS – IF NECESSARY

I conclude that cooperative firms will have to become more polymorphous. Ways will have to be found within existing cooperatives to innovate, particularly as far as procedures for obtaining approval and financial policy are concerned. Alongside this, cooperatives along the lines described by Van der Zwan and Cook will arise. In this atmosphere, we can also observe efforts in the Netherlands to combat the abandonment of agriculture and the loss of jobs in agricultural regions. Take, for example, the environmental cooperatives. They are actually instruments for rural reform and analogous to the traditional cooperative in that they are a correction of the market, be it regional, social or cultural. Just as for the New Generation Cooperatives, members are willing to invest to maintain the rural economy, to generate permanent income and perhaps, too, to preserve a unique style of life.

Justifiably, Van der Zwan points out that direct return on investment is not the only measure to be applied to a cooperative. Members have broader interests. Certainly, those interests are broader than one could expect of shareholders in an investor-owned-firm (IOF). Under these circumstances, perhaps it is better to speak not of return on capital, but of yield on capital. It could be interesting to explore this concept further, and to perhaps even quantify it. However, a broadening of the definition of the concept of return will not change anything for the management of cooperative firms: the same principles and norms hold for those of firms governed by shareholders.

ANNOTATED CLASSIFICATION OF DUTCH COOPERATIVES

The conclusion that there is a trend toward polymorphism among cooperatives may be interesting, but it is hardly concrete. For this reason, I am going to stick my neck out and classify Dutch cooperatives, with the intention of illustrating and even organizing the opinions presented in this book. Through this exercise, I assume readers in other nations will be able to draw similar comparisons with their own organizations.

I intend to use the terminology already established and speak of four generations of cooperatives. But first, I want to warn of a potential misunderstanding: with the exception of the transition of the First Generation Cooperative to the Second Generation Cooperative, there is no succession through to, for example, the Fourth Generation Cooperative as the highest and best form of cooperative culture. Third Generation Cooperatives and Fourth Generation Cooperatives may be younger forms of cooperatives, but they are not the serial progression of the first two.

The First Generation Cooperative is a true extension-cooperative in which cooperative theory and micro-economic theory are concentrated. In the Second Generation Cooperative, the emphasis lies on the firm running one or two cooperative enterprises, striving to implement and balance all the market tools available to it. The Third Generation Cooperative is characterized by the broadening of its objectives, while the Fourth Generation Cooperative embraces a philosophy of development through integrated chain marketing or co-production (co-makership).

FIRST GENERATION COOPERATIVES

The basis of the First Generation Cooperative is market correction. Cooperatives arose as farmers joined forces to counteract (countervailing power) the purchasing and marketing power of monopolies and oligopolies. In raw produce markets, certainly, a bundling or pooling of influence remains important. But more can be done. By developing products that keep better, cooperatives can strengthen their position in current markets as well as open new ones. So the market between farmers and the first stage of processing can be done away with.

The added value of such products is then divided among the members in proportion to their input. During good years, prices rise; in bad years, they fall. Part of the annual performance is earmarked for general reserves (in Dutch, literally the "dead hand") and part is turned into certificates or shares. They remain in the members' account in the cooperative firm. In short, pleasure and pain, just as the contributions to capital formation are proportional to the amount of produce agreed to under contract.

At the heart of the business relationship between members and the cooperative is how members perceive their proportional equity. Often they see it as a cost – not value-added but cost-added. The more efficient the cooperative is, the lower the cost and the greater the return on the capital the members have in the firm. In other words, members strive to maximize the return on their investment in their agricultural firm, which is their farm. The prices paid by the cooperative act as a financial or capital buffer for the cooperative firm. A company pays the going market price to obtain the raw produce it needs. If their sales on the product markets are disappointing, the company's capital forms a buffer for the shortfall.

Production costs in the first phase of production are relatively low. It is the task-oriented organization that keeps a close watch on efficiency, using the latest technology to achieve this. It can also be achieved through mergers and continual improvement of the organizational structure, which can be initiated by either the cooperative's members or its board of directors.

The majority of dairying, meat, potato and livestock transport cooperatives began in this way. Most concentrate on one product or product category. Usually, membership is open to all those who are in the same sector, or the requirements for their eligibility are kept to a minimum. The terms of notice for those wishing to resign from the cooperative are long, or penalties are levied, because the productive capacity of the cooperative firm is directly related to that of the membership. Hence, when members leave, they increase the costs for those remaining. The response is an exit penalty, a barrier to their leaving. In contrast, there is seldom a ceiling on production capacity, irrespective of the artificial market forces of governmental agricultural policies.

The administrative "center of gravity" of the cooperative is the farmers' board; in this board of directors, decisions are made on the basis of one man, one vote. The members' interests are usually divided proportionately, and management has barely any statutory powers.

Nowadays, First Generation Cooperatives are rare. In the Netherlands, all cooperatives have developed into Second Generation Cooperatives or are in the process of doing so. Some have become Fourth Generation Cooperatives, which will be discussed later. As I have already said, the transition to a Second Generation Cooperative is not a decisive change of course, but rather an evolution. It is driven by changes on the demand side of the market and through autonomous growth that follows in the wake of a clear perception of institutional identity, organizational dynamism, and a healthy culture of professionalism.

SECOND GENERATION COOPERATIVES

What are the characteristics of the Second Generation Cooperatives? Why do all the experts interviewed in this book speak of the problems to be encountered in the transition from First Generation Cooperatives to Second Generation Cooperatives?

Second Generation Cooperatives grew from the realization that cooperatives with more market influence must penetrate ever further along the marketing chain, getting closer and closer to the consumer if they intend to maintain a reasonable piece of the value-added "cake." Many an expert in this book have emphasized just this point: in today's markets, cooperatives must deal with bulk buyers and multinational competitors. It is in this setting that the cooperative firm can stand out by developing a variety of products from raw produce that is of consistently high quality.

It can also be achieved through vertically integrating the production processes from the farm gate to the consumer to ensure the quality of special products. The Second Generation Cooperative mirrors the market for farmers: it translates the market for them. That is another means by which the cooperative firm, in particular, can distinguish itself. Such product guarantees, especially reliability and safety, are crucially important for retailers. Hughes is convinced that cooperative firms are best suited to provide such guarantees and security. In modern economic terms, cooperatives can do this for the lowest transaction costs. The fact that demand, rather than supply, is the determining factor here means that exit penalties of the First Generation Cooperative will be replaced by nomination or entry fees. Open membership and unrestricted entry will become the exception rather than the rule.

The members' shares of Avebe, a Dutch farmers' industrial starch cooperative, are linked to the compulsory supply (delivery) of members' industrial-grade potatoes. Members may buy and sell these shares among themselves, or even to new members just entering the cooperative. Share prices will reflect the market performance of the cooperative. In this regard, the value of the cooperative's shares is a response to the success of the firm the same way shares in public stock companies reflect their firms' performance.

Overcapacity, which occurred naturally in First Generation Cooperatives, has virtually disappeared in the dairy sector. Compulsory supply and exit barriers have been transformed into entrance fees and barriers to entry. In Second Generation Cooperatives, differences in price-setting leadership can occur. Campina Melkunie, for example, has accepted this leadership. Prices remain a reflection of the performance of the firm. Nevertheless, efforts are being made to find ways to create permanent forms of raising risk-bearing capital from among members. The return on that investment will be determined by the capital market. Under tight fiscal policies, it remains extremely difficult to attract permanent risk-bearing capital.

Friesland Dairy Foods (FDF) is traditionally active on international markets, especially those outside the European Union. FDF is gradually transforming these activities into international firms. The members remain owners of these firms, but they do not supply them with raw produce nor are they involved with their management.

A Second Generation Cooperative, FDF is different than Campina Melkunie. FDF does not link the price it pays members for their milk to the returns on investment of its international activities. That price would reflect incorrect economic information given the globalization that FDF has already accomplished. There would be no relationship between the price paid for milk and its supply by members. The realized performance of the firm is determined as much by international business as by business on the basis of members' milk supplies. It is for this reason that FDF has rejected the role of price leader. Members are paid a price based on the five best-paying firms in the Netherlands. To acquire capital, FDF offers its members shares which can be traded freely amongst each other. The firm's performance is reflected in the returns per share and prices of the shares.

The governance structure of Second Generation Cooperatives is different from First Generation Cooperatives in the Netherlands. Second Generation firms operate like an investor-owned firm. The relationship between the supervisory body, the board of governors, and the management is also different to that of the First Generation Cooperative. For the Second Generation Cooperative, this relationship is similar to that of commercial trading companies that are not cooperatives.

Some of the external forces that have encouraged the transition in the Netherlands from a First Generation Cooperative to a Second Generation Cooperative have led elsewhere to completely different organizations forms. The evolution of some of the dairy cooperatives in Ireland into PLCs (Public Limited Companies) are among the most striking examples of this. In the early Nineties, several Irish cooperatives decided to make use of risk-bearing capital from outsiders and so registered themselves on the stock exchange. In the majority of these new PLCs, most of the share capital remained in the hands of the original members. Nevertheless, the characteristics typical of cooperatives have disappeared from these firms. Conversely, other cooperatives elsewhere in Ireland were preserving and even strengthening their cooperative nature, particularly in their leadership in setting milk prices.

None of the agribusiness cooperatives in the Netherlands have taken this route as yet. It is legally possible for them to do so, however, as has been shown by the pharmaceutical wholesaling company OPG. This cooperative, owned by prescribing chemists (pharmacists), transformed itself into a company registered on the stock exchange in the early Nineties.

THIRD GENERATION COOPERATIVES

I have already mentioned Third Generation Cooperatives, but in this form of enterprise, the aim is to relate consumer demand for specific product groups to the specific skills and specialties of the members. In effect, these cooperatives are a new, sensitive mechanism for linking supply and demand with distinct – regional or otherwise – chains. They may, for example, be based on a particular specialty or level of quality; or, perhaps, niche markets such as organic farming.

Characteristics of such cooperatives, which originated in the United States, reflect a broadening of goals (rural prosperity, employment); the integration of production and ownership (investment); and closed membership. So far, this form of cooperative is relatively unknown in the Netherlands. But a variant, "environmental cooperatives," do exist that attempt to correct shortcomings in governmental policies and regulations while preserving natural, landscape and agricultural resources in their regions.

BETWEEN THE SECOND AND FOURTH GENERATION

To describe the Fourth Generation Cooperative, I look to the example of the meat sector where, in 1995, two cooperatives merged with a private firm and thereby radically changed the nature of those cooperatives. The market for pork has been Europe-wide for many years. Dutch pigs are exported live, for example, to Stuttgart, Germany, if the price there is attractive. Cooperatives in this sector have been unable to maintain compulsory supplies from members at pig prices linked to the market performance of the cooperative.

Seen from another point of view, this means the cooperatives could no longer maintain leadership in price setting. The reasons put forward for this vary. I see it as the result of clinging to a First Generation Cooperative mentality for too long – in the sense that the cooperatives accepted over-production conditions much longer than the private companies. Adding to this, an element of bureaucracy crept in, increasing administration costs.

In their new situation, the member-suppliers no longer hold the majority of the firm's shares. Other cooperatives (primarily livestock cooperatives), private companies and special-interest groups hold approximately 70 percent of the shares. The price leadership so integral to the concept of First Generation Cooperatives has disappeared. The pork market can be considered "perfect," (competition exists) thus the cooperative no longer has a corrective role to play in the market.

The cooperative acts in the market as a commercial company, ensuring a share of that market for its members' produce. In such a situation, the firm's profit, its return on investment and the dividend payable on shares are established in the same manner as for any other company.

The cooperative's members participate in the company through their cooperative. As such, they and the company are co-producers. Members who are willing to accept the price leadership of the company for three cycles (approximately one year) and are willing to comply with its terms of supply receive a co-producer's reimbursement. This is a reward for contributing to reducing the transaction costs through fulfilling the supply contract; the price of the raw produce is no longer negotiated. The cooperative then converts the co-producer's reimbursement – a co-maker's fee – into shares which are put at the disposal of the cooperative. The cooperative also maintains a market for member equity. A fund is available so farmers who are closing their farms can sell their capital "rights" for their nominal value if they are unable to obtain better value in the market among members.

I would call this a Fourth Generation Cooperative. It is a safety net for the unsuccessful Second Generation Cooperative. The co-producers reimbursement creates the same relationship that was taken for granted in the First Generation Cooperative.

The foundation of the First Generation Cooperative was trust – "united we stand, divided we fall" – which made the farmers one. In the Second Generation Cooperative, that trust is extended to the undertaking of ventures further along the agricultural-produce chain. That trust is absent in the Fourth Generation Cooperative as its basis – the need for countervailing power – is too weak. The relationship with members is formalized through a contract in the Fourth Generation Cooperative. The cooperative remains as the organization in which farmers are guaranteed the opportunity to develop their farming skills. But a contract is signed annually to seal the relationship.

In the future, it is quite likely we will witness the transformation of Fourth Generation Cooperatives into Second Generation Cooperatives, and vice versa.

COMMUNICATION WITHIN THE CHAIN

To achieve a permanent place in the food processing chain, in combination with a variety of roles in relation to the rural economy, the differing economies of scale that occur in agriculture will have to be well integrated. Cooperation is the key to all of this. The different analyses presented in this book make it clear that there are two important issues involved: the relationship between large cooperatives and international markets, and communication between large cooperatives and their members.

There is general agreement that scaling up and internationalization are necessary to preserve the classical countervailing power of cooperatives against competitors and the increasing concentration of retailing chains. Control of the distribution chain – an important contribution from Hughes – is growing in importance as *the factor* in the power equation.

Down the chain – and it is here where the ideas of Van der Zwan are so valuable – there is a growing realization that scaling up and internationalization are leading to a growing imbalance in the relationship between supply and demand, and employment prospects at the local level. The challenge as Van der Zwan sees it is to redefine the bargain by which the cooperative participates in the market on behalf of its members (for which the members bear the risk). Farmers – second to none as a group in the ferocity with which they are willing to fight for their own survival – are innovative pioneers suitable for this task.

EXPECTATION AND VALUES

In addition to business aspects, the expectation and values of the members play a crucial role in the cooperative. With this in mind, In 't Veld points out that a cooperative may be forced to embrace one set of values at a certain point in time. With that reminder, it is striking that almost every contributor to this book points to the need for effective and efficient supervision of management by the members. This is to ensure that the cooperative is run to meet the members' aims, not simply to look over its shoulders to prevent business mistakes.

What, then, are the values that bind members, and how can they be met? Strategic policies – for example, scaling up, international ventures or vertical integration – must be judged against the aims of the cooperative's members.

That sounds simple, but that is hardly the case. It is here where problems lay for the Second Generation Cooperatives. In particular, it is from here that the conflict between short- and long-term interests stems; as well as the divergence of managing the effects of external forces on the cooperative and the privately-owned firm.

It is that difference that makes intensive, structurally well-organized communications essential to cooperatives. Professor Roel in 't Veld points out that cooperative values can be influenced by strategic decisions. Thus, the value "hedge against risk" acquires a new significance as the level of entrepreneurial risk increases. Similarly, solidarity with a farmer-neighbor takes on another meaning in an internationally-oriented cooperative. Of great value is the advice that not only managers but also farmer-directors should be willing to bring in consultants to help formulate and evaluate business strategy. This is widely practiced in the Netherlands. For my part, I should like to emphasize the virtual indispensability of the instruments of education, information and training for board members. I am absolutely convinced that too little attention is paid to them.

These and the other instruments discussed in this book are necessary to preserve the essence of the cooperative tradition. It is this tradition that leads the most prophetic of the participating experts to view cooperatives as one of the most obvious answers to the social issues of tomorrow. The exact nature of such an answer cannot be predicted, but I expect the Netherlands will play a pioneering role in finding it. Perhaps the readers of this book from various nations will arrive at the same conclusion and seek their own answers. What an encouraging and challenging idea!

INDEX

B

C

English Edition Design: Lone Oak Press
Graphics by Marisa Egerstrom

Photography: Duane Dailey, Artifolio Veenendaal B. V.,
Andy King, Th. Cheska, Philip Baile, Atilji Euhlund,
Joseph Angeles, Hansen, Henk Tukker, Bert Houweling

Translation of original Dutch to English provided by
Cressie Communication Services,
Graaf Ottolaan 15, 6861 BS
Oosterbeek, The Netherlands.